P9-CKR-941

WITHDRAWN

Praise for *The Myth of the Dying Church*

"The wonderful thing about Glenn Stanton's new book is that it demonstrates Christ's promise that he is the author and finisher of our faith. It is a call to stop trusting ourselves as the saviors of the world and to rejoice in the truth that God has got it under control. In gratitude for this immeasurable gift, his book calls us to rededicate ourselves to faithful parenting and neighborly charity."

Joy Pullmann

Executive editor, *The Federalist*,
and mom of five little ones

"If you're a parent, you've likely been shaken by reports that young people are abandoning Christianity in droves and growing up to be aimless, faithless adults. But take heart—much of what you've heard and read in this regard is simply not true. In *The Myth of the Dying Church*, Glenn Stanton takes a hard look at the evidence and finds that Christianity is alive and well, even flourishing."

Jim Daly

President, Focus on the Family

"In *The Myth of the Dying Church*, Glenn Stanton challenges some commonly held assumptions about the spiritual practices and beliefs of Christians today. This book is not only insightful and balanced, but positive and hopeful. It is a must-read for anyone concerned with the state of the church today. Based on extensive research, Stanton offers practical advice for engaging our wider culture and raising up a new generation of Christ followers."

Sean McDowell, Ph.D.

Professor, Biola University

"In these turbulent and uncertain times, Christians are given to imbibing every depressing media tidbit that prophesies the continued shrinking of the church and eventual demise of the faith. This is why I am delighted to see Glenn Stanton's new book, *The Myth of the Dying Church*. Utilizing today's leading social scientific research, Stanton offers us a more judicious and promising assessment of the state of the Christian faith in North America and around the world. More importantly, he paints a compelling picture of the church's future—one that is grounded in reality and yet elevated by the resilient hope that we have in the gospel. Highly recommend!"

Todd Wilson

President, Center for Pastor Theologians

"Is Christianity declining? Glenn Stanton challenges this dominant narrative, and it's about time. Stanton is not simply looking at our situation with rose-colored glasses, but providing a perspective often missing today—that of how Christianity is not really receding. There are challenges, as he documents. The fuzzy middle is certainly shrinking. But after you dismiss the hysteria, there are obvious and truly meaningful reasons for hope. Read it and be encouraged."

Mark Regnerus, Ph.D.

Professor of sociology, University of Texas at Austin

"Is Christianity on the wane? Many say so, but this book, with much evidence, argues to the contrary. Accommodated Christianity is in deep decline, but gospel-focused churches are still vibrant and growing explosively around the globe. This study is both a source of encouragement and a summons to faithfulness."

Timothy George

Founding dean, Beeson Divinity School, Samford University, and general editor, Reformation Commentary on Scripture series

"Everything you thought you knew about the decline of Christianity in the modern world is wrong. That's the conclusion Glenn Stanton reaches after combing through dozens of studies by the most well-respected scholars. What's really happening is that *some* churches are declining (those that teach a liberal theology), while *others* are growing (those that teach an orthodox theology). The same pattern holds not only in the United States but around the globe. Stanton has done a great service by pulling together the findings of a wide range of researchers. If you've been despondent over the state of Christianity, you will find much in this book to encourage you."

Nancy Pearcey
Author of *Total Truth* and *Love Thy Body*

"Glenn Stanton has continually and bravely challenged mainstream thinking on cultural issues. In *The Myth of the Dying Church* he uses reliable social science survey data to refute the myth that the contemporary American evangelical church is shrinking. Indeed, he provides robust evidence that the American church continues to thrive in the face of its imperfections and challenges. Kudos for this timely and important book."

Bruce Wydick
Professor of economics and international studies,
University of San Francisco

"What if Jesus *really* meant it when He said the gates of hell would not prevail against His church? What if the sky isn't falling? Glenn Stanton has a knack for looking at the data and getting past the headlines. In *The Myth of the Dying Church*, he allows us to see clearly the gift God has given the world in His ever-expanding church."

John Stonestreet
President, Chuck Colson Center for Christian Worldview

"Those of you irritated by the glee with which secularists and atheists announce the looming death of religion in general and Christianity in particular need to read this book. The predictors have it wrong. Religion isn't dying. It's holding steady, and in some important cases it's increasing. As Glenn Stanton shows, it all depends on how you define *religion*, and what message you want to deliver. Secularists desperately want to envision a dying church, but it's a myth. Stanton's deliciously ironic conclusion is this: it's the anti-religionists who are captive to an illusion, not the believers!"

Mark Bauerlein

Senior editor, *First Things*,

professor of English, Emory University

"Is Christianity really dying in America? Glenn Stanton says 'No!' in his intriguing new book, *The Myth of the Dying Church*. His evidence, observations, and recommendations for mission should be seriously considered. Not only is it important that Christians discern truth from falsehood in media coverage of the church; it is imperative that we understand the mission field globally and locally so we may be the wiser laborers in the Lord's harvest. His fresh voice demands our attention."

James M. Kushiner

Executive editor, *Touchstone: A Journal of Mere Christianity*

"In stark contrast to the usual humdrum of decline, defeat, and surrender, Glenn Stanton writes with an unusual breath of fresh air that leaves the reader both exhilarated and motivated. It's time to double down on what you know is true: Jesus has risen, He is in control, and His church is thriving. Get ready—you are going to love this book."

Wayne Mulqueen

National director for Focus on the Family New Zealand

"Glenn Stanton may be my favorite Christian cultural analyst. He combines faithfulness with winsomeness and clear thinking. While I appreciate him as a friend, I trust him as an analyst and interpreter of ideas and data. During a time when we are regularly bombarded with reports of religious decline, Glenn Stanton can be relied upon to dive deep beneath the headlines and deliver the straight story."

Hunter Baker, J.D., Ph.D.
Author of *The End of Secularism* and
dean of arts and sciences at Union University

"Is the church in decline? Pollsters and journalists—even some Christian leaders—cherry-pick data to make us believe the answer to that question is YES. Glenn Stanton answers that question with a resounding, encouraging NO. His case is convincing. He says church attendance is at an all-time high. Young people are not abandoning the church. Around the world, Christianity is booming. This book is a much-needed corrective to shoddy thinking and anti-Biblical preaching and teaching in today's evangelical church."

Warren Cole Smith
Vice president, Mission Advancement,
the Colson Center for Christian Worldview

THE
MYTH
OF THE DYING
CHURCH

HOW CHRISTIANITY IS ACTUALLY THRIVING
IN AMERICA AND THE WORLD

GLENN T. STANTON

WORTHY®
PUBLISHING

New York • Nashville

Copyright © 2019 by Glenn T. Stanton
Cover copyright © 2019 by Hachette Book Group, Inc.

Hachette Book Group supports the right to free expression and the value of copyright. The purpose of copyright is to encourage writers and artists to produce the creative works that enrich our culture.

The scanning, uploading, and distribution of this book without permission is a theft of the author's intellectual property. If you would like permission to use material from the book (other than for review purposes), please contact permissions@hbgusa.com. Thank you for your support of the author's rights.

Worthy
Hachette Book Group
1290 Avenue of the Americas, New York, NY 10104

worthypublishing.com
twitter.com/worthypub

First Edition: June 2019

Worthy is a division of Hachette Book Group, Inc. The Worthy name and logo are trademarks of Hachette Book Group, Inc.

The publisher is not responsible for websites (or their content) that are not owned by the publisher.

Scripture quotations are taken from the ESV® Bible (The Holy Bible, English Standard Version®), copyright © 2001 by Crossway, a publishing ministry of Good News Publishers. Used by permission. All rights reserved.

Cover design by Bill Chiaravalle | Brand Navigation
Print book interior design by Bart Dawson

Cataloging-in-Publication Data is on file with the Library of Congress.

ISBNs: 978-1-68397-305-8 (hardcover), 978-1-54601-516-1 (ebook)

Printed in the United States of America
LSC-C
10 9 8 7 6 5 4 3 2 1

To all faithful and hardworking pastors.
You are the bride's most important attendant.
Thank you for your sacrifice and service.

CONTENTS

"[L]et it be your pleasure to remember that the Church
is an anvil which has worn out many a hammer."
Theodore Beza, John Calvin's Successor

"And I tell you, you are Peter, and on this rock I will build my church,
and the gates of hell shall not prevail against it."
Matthew 16:18

"And the Lord added to their number day by day
those who were being saved."
Acts 2:47

"After this I looked, and behold, a great multitude that no one
could number, from every nation, from all tribes and peoples
and languages, standing before the throne and before the Lamb."
Revelation 7:9

FOREWORD

In *The Myth of the Dying Church*, Glenn Stanton forcefully argues against the notion churches in the United States are in dramatic decline. Stanton carefully reviews scholarly publications that, taken together, provide compelling empirical evidence about the health of churches that is vastly different from the narrative commonly asserted in the media and, yes, regrettably preached from many church pulpits—that churches are dying in America while atheism is on the rise. This book provides a well-documented and much needed corrective.

Stanton correctly points out that there is indeed a dramatic decline among some American churches, but this severe decline can be found in a distinct group of churches found within theologically liberal mainline Protestantism. The well-documented decline of mainline churches has been decades in the making and continues to the present. Despite this fact, we regularly hear that all churches are shrinking or, worse, closing altogether. Indeed, a recent and terribly flawed *Atlantic Monthly* article entitled "America's Epidemic of

Empty Churches" does nothing but confirm what Stanton and others have found: it is liberal churches that are in decline and closing.

On the other hand, theologically conservative denominations (evangelical churches, Pentecostal churches, and especially non-denominational churches) are not in decline but are alive and well. Stanton does an excellent job of explaining in an accessible way why the headlines continue to get it wrong. *The Myth of the Dying Church* is must reading for another reason. It helps us understand why Americans—religious as well as non-religious—benefit from the very fact that so many of the churches in the United States are not in decline but thriving. Here's the explanation:

Over the last several decades, thousands of studies published in peer-reviewed journals document that the practice of attending church is associated with making people happier, healthier, better spouses, more generous, more ethical, more tolerant, and more civically engaged and responsible citizens. Thus, even non-religious people who do not attend church are passive recipients of the benefit of those who do regularly attend. And yet there is even more good news. Active church goers are more likely to experience better physical and mental health. Other studies have examined how religious participation is linked to educational achievement, character development, longevity, coping, and stress reduction. Still other research demonstrates how church attendance can help decrease crime and delinquency, and how religious practices help increase sobriety among addicts in treatment. Scholars have also assessed the conditions under which religious involvement in congregations enhances social capital and networks of social support that aid human flourishing. In sum, there is a significant body of empirical evidence in the form of thousands of published studies that demonstrate the ways in which church attendance is linked to a host of protective factors as well as prosocial outcomes.

Finally, it is important to note that many vibrant churches provide a host of social services to the neighborhoods where they are located. These churches assumed to be dying actually provide support to a host of faith-based organizations (e.g., Salvation Army, Catholic Charities, substance abuse centers, pregnancy resource centers, Gospel Rescue Missions, Compassion International, etc.) that have been part of public life for decades and provide social service delivery for over seventy million Americans annually.

Sociologist Brian Grim designed an innovative study published in 2016, which provides a preliminary but plausible estimate of the economic contribution of religion to American society. Drawing from a host of different data sources, Grim provides initial estimates that religion contributes approximately $1.2 trillion to the U.S. economy each year. Thus, the implications of what Stanton presents here has larger ramifications than just how many people are attending church each week. They accentuate how the strength and vibrancy of the church today has vast consequences, impacting personal and societal well-being for everyone.

Relying upon empirical evidence rather than anecdotes, *The Myth of the Dying Church* sets the record straight on what we know about churches in America. This book should be required reading for seminary students and anyone interested in gaining a better understanding of the role and vitality of churches in America, and the faith that motivates them.

Byron R. Johnson, Ph.D.
Director, Institute for Studies of Religion
Distinguished Professor of the Social Sciences
Baylor University

INTRODUCTION

WHAT YOU'VE BEEN TOLD IS TRUE . . . IS NOT

Do you know what one of the biggest lies about the church is today? It's actually been going around for a number of years now. You may have even innocently passed along this false information to others. After all, you've received your information from reliable resources—pastors and other Christian leaders, authors and the news media, pollsters. They proclaim often and with great confidence that the number of people who claim to be Christians is shrinking drastically while the number of "nones" (those who are religiously unaffiliated) is growing like weeds. Therefore, the church will soon disappear.

This news is certainly disturbing to all who love Jesus and His church and who desire to spread the life-giving gospel. Even more alarming, though, is how many Christians have bought this news as truth and allowed it to weaken their faith and put their churches on the defensive (if not cause them to lie down and wait to die).

But I have good news for you: IT'S SIMPLY NOT TRUE!

It is important to understand what is really, truly happening with the church today. In this book, I explore and present in an understandable way data from leading academic sources today that provides a broad array of the best evidence for significant hopefulness. Our exploration will also help us understand how and why so many smart and well-intentioned people have gotten it so wrong in their understanding of the state of the church today.

Let me provide you with a quick summary of the truth on the matter in plain language:

1. Liberal churches are hemorrhaging members. Churches that are bailing on Christian orthodoxy—those denying the deity of Christ; rejecting the reality of sin; doubting the historical reality of Christ's death and resurrection; and embracing abortion, gay, and gender politics—are all in a drastic free fall. People are leaving those churches as though the buildings were on fire. They can't get out fast enough.

2. Biblical churches are holding strong. Churches that are faithfully preaching, teaching, and practicing biblical truths and conservative theology are holding stable overall. Some are seeing steady growth and others are exploding. No small number are pressed thin with the good problem of figuring out how to manage their growing crowds. You likely know of a few in your own community; perhaps you even attend one of these churches.

3. Church attendance is at an all-time high. More Americans, in raw numbers and as a percentage of the population, attend church today than at any other time in our nation's history, including the colonial days. That's hardly scary news.

4. More young adults attend biblically faithful churches today than attended nearly fifty years ago. According to some of the best sociological data, the percentage of young adults regularly attending evangelical and nondenominational churches has roughly doubled between 1972 and today.

5. Atheism and agnosticism are not growing wildly. Both have grown in the last few years, but they are an extreme minority, counting for just about 7 percent of all US adults.

6. The Nones are not new unbelievers. The infamous "nones"—those reporting to have no particular institutional faith—are indeed a growing category. This has been widely reported. But there is something *very* important to note here: they are not a new category. They are *not* folks who have left a once living faith but rather are those who merely had a cold or lukewarm family history of church identity and now feel more comfortable saying, "I don't really identify with anything." It's not a change in belief. Instead, it's an honest explanation for where they've always been.

7. Global growth of Christianity is booming. The number of Christians in the world today is larger than it has ever been in the history of the world and will continue to increase through the coming decades. The story here is incredibly positive. Scholars studying this phenomenon use words like *explosive* and *mushrooming* to describe Christianity's global growth, particularly in China and Southern Asia, Africa, and South America.

These things describe the true state of the Christian faith in both America and around the world as recorded by leading sociologists of religion who employ an array of different means to study the phenomenon and who have no particular commitment or interest in reaching any specific finding. They are simply looking at the numbers as honestly as they can and reporting their findings. This book tells the story of these findings—examining important details, uncovering critical nuances, and explaining how conclusions are reached—and what it all means for the future of Jesus's church and its life-giving mission in the world.

Here is the path we will take in our exploration. First, we will set up the situation and consider the different claims made by various voices predicting Christianity's impending demise to see how sensational so much of it is. Next, over a number of chapters, we will carefully examine the breadth of fascinating research showing where church growth and decline are taking place and how proper interpretation tells a very hopeful story both in terms of which churches and traditions are shrinking and which are growing.

We then examine some extremely encouraging research on how it's very possible for parents to successfully pass on their faith to their children by providing a few basic experiences for their children. In fact, it's very likely most parents who do these things will succeed in raising kids with an enduring faith. Doing so is not rocket science, there's no secret formula, nor is it a crapshoot. It's relatively simple, and any parent can do it regardless of education, income, or spiritual maturity. Parents don't even have to do it perfectly. How encouraging is that?

We will also take a quick look at how so many good and smart people could come to the wrong conclusions and how these conclusions have taken a deep root in the media and our collective conscience. As we will learn, anyone interested in the truth should not rely on one study here or another there—which most people reporting bad news unfortunately do—but should consider the larger collection of research conducted by reputable sociologists of religion and polling organizations.

Next, we will observe how the gospel spreads from generation to generation and how the Holy Spirit, who has been directing us in all truth and animating and empowering the church since the day of Pentecost, is certainly not asleep at the wheel. He is not on vacation,

He has not weakened, and the gates of hell will not prevail against Christ's church—just as Jesus promised in Matthew 16:18. This is perhaps the most important thing we must grasp here.

We will end by looking at the future of the Christian faith and what we all need from the church as it goes forth into the world with the life-giving and world-changing power of the gospel.

Let me be very clear on an important note. I am not claiming that everything is all hunky-dory for the church today. There are many issues of concern, such as declines in basic biblical and theological knowledge and in an essential Christian worldview. There are increases in a consumer-oriented, entertainment-driven Christian culture in the West. Too much teaching and preaching in the church and Christian media today is merely self-help theory dressed up with Bible verses. But there are many positive signs as well. So, all in all, I have very good news for you: the sky is not falling, and that's the story I am going to tell you here.

CHAPTER 1

IS CHICKEN LITTLE RIGHT?

P oor Chicken Little.

She freaked out about nearly everything and cried constantly about the apocalyptic doom that was going to rain down upon everyone's heads, literally.[1] But in reality, the sky wasn't falling at all. It was just an acorn submitting to the everyday laws of gravity and landing on Chicken Little's soft cranial palate that caused her hysteria. Of course, she doesn't keep the freak-out to herself. And it spreads like a cold, as freak-outs are inclined to do.

On her way to warn the king about this terrible news, she bumps into all her rhyming-named woodland friends—Foxy Loxy, Turkey Lurkey, Henny Penny, Goosey Loosey, and the rest of the crew—and alerts them of the coming Armageddon. They take her pronouncement unquestionably as truth and all join in the hysterics, spreading the disconcerting news to the whole village.

This famous folktale has been told from generation to generations across many countries for well over a hundred and fifty years because it speaks to a global truth. Bad news, even when false, travels fast. Of course, this story has a very direct correlation to the reported steep decline and impending demise of the Christian church. On this topic there are far too many Chicken Littles today, and their tale of the falling-acorn-turned-Armageddon has unfortunately become unquestioned and indisputable fact as they claim the following for all to hear and fear:

> Christianity is shrinking, and most are joining the ranks of the nones, especially the young people. Buses leaving hourly. Commence the hysteria.

Nearly everyone has played along, basing their opinions on a few news reports and claims from people who seem like authorities and make their statements with absolute confidence. Few take the time to dig further into the story and consult multiple sources in order to determine whether such news holds up. However, this is what detectives do—and what all good reporters once did—but most people today don't have the time or resources to do such deep digging for themselves. That is precisely why I wrote this book. I wanted to do the digging and look at a vast array of deeply informed academic sources so I could explain the truth of the situation in clear and simple ways to help Christians, church staff, journalists, and thought leaders understand the important angles and nuances of the bigger picture.

As we will see, the facts don't support the doom-and-gloom story the news media and many Christian leaders are reporting. There are, indeed, positive sides to the story if one reads beyond the headlines and summaries; many are *very* positive. An absolute wealth of information is available that tells a whole different story.

But before we address the important question of what's true about Christianity today, we must look at what the Chicken Littles have been saying. Their tales of an impending demise of the church come in two forms: general and specific.

The general claim made is that Christianity has been declining dramatically over the last decade, with people simply losing interest in it and going elsewhere. This storyline is featured in endless publications with actual headlines such as these:

- *Washington Post*: "Christianity Faces Sharp Decline as Americans Are Becoming Even Less Affiliated with Religion"
- *Newsmax*: "Christianity Declines Sharply in US, Agnostics Growing: Pew"
- *Atlantic*: "America's Empty Church Problem"
- BeliefNet: "Declining Christianity: The Exodus of the Young and the Rise of Atheism"
- National Public Radio: "Christians in U.S. on Decline as Number of 'Nones' Grows, Survey Finds"
- *New York Times*: "Big Drop in Share of Americans Calling Themselves Christian"
- *Huffington Post*: "America Is Getting Less Christian and Less Religious, Study Shows"

Sometime back in the late 2000s, while the US was experiencing a deep decline in new car sales, which initiated the massive federal bailout of the auto industry, a Christian leader[2] famously said that if current trends kept up, most churches would look exactly like these deserted, tumbleweed-strewn car lots that were gracing the front pages of nearly every newspaper. Rather than the choirs, worship teams, and raucous bustles of youth groups, we were told to expect the chirping of crickets and cobwebs within the wall of most churches. You can't get any more "the sky is falling" than that, can you?

A book reviewer for the *New York Times* made this assertion with absolute confidence in 2000:

> Visit a church at random next Sunday and you will probably encounter a few dozen people sprinkled thinly over a sanctuary that was built to accommodate hundreds or even thousands. The empty pews and white-haired congregants lend credence to those who argue that traditional religious worship is dying out. . . . But the traditional church . . . has failed to present religion in a style that the modern world could accept and understand—and has lost touch with the evangelistic impulse that built the great congregations in the first place. To put it in business terms, the traditional church has failed to protect its franchise and its market share.[3]

This is a very stark picture indeed, the church on its last leg, gasping out its final breath. Someone call for last rites.

Christian Smith, one of the world's leading sociologists of

religion, examines growth and belief trends in the Christian church, and he has been long concerned about this false hysteria. He told of one whopper he saw some years ago in an advertisement in a prominent Christian magazine. The ad was for a major evangelical leadership conference, and it proclaimed that Christianity in America wouldn't survive another decade unless we did something *now*. Interestingly enough, attending that conference was exactly what the church needed to do *now*. How about that for motivation? "Attend this conference and save Christianity in our nation, or live with the guilt that you allowed it to shrivel up and die." That was basically the message being communicated. Smith, in good fun, hoped that someone had let God know of this terrible future.[4] Let us note that that supposed decade of doom has now past, and here we still are.

No one should take these kinds of claims seriously. My church is still around, and the pews are still crowded. My friends' churches still exist. I pass churches on a daily basis that have loads of cars in their parking lots on Sunday mornings and weeknight evenings.

Yes, some churches are struggling, and even declining. Others are aging and unable to connect with younger generations, and still others have faced crises with church staff and church splits. But these are not due to a "Christian recession" but simply because of issues within those particular churches, which is an important distinction. I'll bet a week's worth of lunch money that your church is chugging along well. The odds are totally in my favor. We all need to be more informed to know the truth in this area. Christians are born again, but we shouldn't act like we were born yesterday.

The other Chicken Little narrative is more specific, concerning our own children and their friends. It claims some of them—if not most of them—are highly unlikely to hang on to their faith as they get older. Try as you might, good and faithful Christian parents, but your efforts to pass on your faith to your children are going to fail. Countless blog articles and books published by Christian leaders espouse this, often based on their own research. Here are examples:

- Leading Christian author: "Young people are leaving the church in droves," reflected in "staggering numbers" of those who say they no longer believe.
- Major Christian magazine advertisement: "This generation of teens is the largest in history—and current trends show that only 4 percent will be evangelical believers by the time they become adults. Compare this with 34 percent of adults today who are evangelicals. We are on the verge of a catastrophe."
- Newsletter from a parachurch organization: "Up to 90 percent or more of Christian kids will leave the church by the time they reach adulthood."
- Headline from an evangelical research company report: "Most Twenty-Somethings Put Christianity on the Shelf Following Spiritually Active Teen Years"
- Youth ministry publication: "86% of evangelical youth drop out of church after graduation, never to return."
- Well-known teacher at a major evangelical school: "According to present trends, we are about to eternally lose the second largest generation in America's history."

- Advertisement for a book: Young adults who are leaving the church are "a black hole" in contemporary Christianity.

Seriously? A *black hole*? A sucking, gaping hole of nothingness that pulls everything around it into utter darkness? Please! Chicken Little would be green with envy at such dramatics. To make it all worse, statements regarding a supposed decline of Christianity are usually preceded with the confident admission, "As we all know, Christianity in our nation is . . ." Surely you can easily name similar examples that have gotten your attention and caused you no small amount of angst. Unfortunately they are not hard to find.

At the risk of sounding irreverent, God must be totally freaking out over this news. For the first time since Pentecost, His gospel—not to mention the unquenchable Holy Spirit—seems to be failing to penetrate an entire generation. Christ's church is like a 2008 pre-bailout car lot! Empty pews, with only a smattering of white-haired congregants! The youth, a black hole!

As we will see in chapter 11, we must realize that buying this terribly bad news has huge implications for our understanding of and confidence in how God actually works through the history of His church. Believing that the church is dying impacts how we comprehend the beauty of His irresistible grace and the power of His hand to reach into our communities, not to mention His sovereignty. That hand is unspeakably more powerful than these headlines and the supposed statistics behind them allow for. The Holy Spirit is not walking with a limp or asleep at the wheel.

Professor Bradley R. E. Wright, a noted sociologist at the University of Connecticut—and an evangelical Christian—has studied faith trends among old and young adults over the generations and categorically rejects the Chicken Little scenario. He says it's easy to refute these dire predictions and put the entire situation into perspective by simply looking at recent spiritual giants and their impact on recent generations.

Like Professor Wright, I'm a child of the 1970s, and our generation early on was not a group of thriving Christian stalwarts, by any measure. The generation before us? The hippies. There were all turning on, tuning in, and dropping out, as Timothy Leary famously put it. They didn't inspire any confidence in the future from their own parents or nearly any other adults. If these kids paid any attention to Jesus at all, He was a "groovy cat" who drifted from place to place, with His robe, long hair, and leather sandals, begging for food and talking about peace, love, and understanding. The original hippie. There was every reason to be concerned about the future of the church, if not society as whole, in the hands of this generation.

But as this generation entered early adulthood, thousands of them began to lead one of the largest periods of growth in evangelical history and one of the most powerful moves of God in the past one hundred years: the Jesus movement, of which I'm a very grateful beneficiary. Many of these shaggy-haired, torn jeans–wearing, sandal-shod, rock 'n' roll–playing young people grew to be extremely influential pastors who have preached God's Word with great clarity and truthfulness. They ended up calling people to an obedient discipleship, teaching evangelism, and leading explosively growing churches. Greg Laurie, Rick Warren, and Franklin Graham are but three representative examples. There are hundreds more. This was the generation that initiated the phenomenon of the *megachurch*, which we will examine later. They ushered in the remarkably influential contemporary Christian music scene through artists such as Larry Norman, Love Song, Phil Keaggy, Keith Green, Randy Stonehill, 2nd Chapter of Acts, Resurrection Band, Petra, and Mustard Seed Faith, just to name a few.

More extremely effectual leaders continued to come along after them, and the church continues to grow in important sectors today. The church establishment of the early 1960s never would have put a plug nickel on that shaggy bunch of youngsters, and they were proven wrong. Dramatically so! God is in the business of doing remarkable things in confounding ways with very unlikely people.

It is a sociological truism that what one generation is today in its youth is often not what it grows up to be. As an interesting aside, do the math on the BMW-driving yuppies, 1980s DINKs, and the Reagan generation who came to dominate the American scene. Hint: They were in their teens during the late 1960s and early '70s. In the history of mankind, it is the rare generation of adults who thought the next generation of youth was set to usher in a brighter future of faith, fidelity, and fortune. Today is no different. "Kids these days" is an ancient and ever-present phrase representing the uneasiness and anxiety of the "get off my lawn" adults.

Over the coming chapters, we will explore what the best and larger body of serious research says about the state of the church today. It's a remarkable story, and one that is actually much more exciting and hopeful than I expected to find when I started the research for this book.

CHAPTER 2

THE TRUTH IS MUCH MORE HOPEFUL THAN YOU THINK

The answer to the question of whether Christianity is shrinking or not is both yes and no. This seemingly contradictory answer is the key to understanding the truth of the current and future state of the church. But for a people of faith committed to truth and used to dealing in the absolute categories of black and white, right and wrong, true and false, how can we accept the right answer being two clear opposites?

Let's get to examining what the best data actually shows, and we'll see how the numbers reveal the real guts and truth of the story. In a few words, the story is this:

Some parts of the church are indeed shrinking and some are not at all. Some are doing quite well, even growing. But which parts of the church are shrinking and to what degree? And which churches are doing well?

These are the two fundamental questions. Let me explain our path of exploration in the coming chapters as we examine the research. We will move across the lake from the shore of confusion to the opposite shore of clarity, stepping on the orderly stones that are the findings of the most notable professional research, journal articles, and reports from leading mainstream organizations that track church growth and decline numbers. We won't rely on news stories or organizations that are identified with a particular faith tradition. We will not be relying on one or two sources, the common problem in most reporting on and retelling of this story. We will be taking a much wider, deeper approach and get up to our elbows in the mixing bowl of this research, but in a very readable, direct, and easy-to-understand way.

To employ another metaphor here, like students on a guided tour, we will stop by, be introduced to, and check in with the essential original voices and leading experts on our topic to see what they have to teach us. This is really the only way we can get the actual, reliable picture of things.

Let's start by considering the investigative work of two widely respected leaders in this field of study: Greg Smith and Rodney Stark.

Greg Smith has long worked as the associate director of research for the Pew Research Center, one of the most trusted and respected institutions on this topic. In an interview with *Christianity Today* a few years ago, Smith was asked by Dr. Ed Stetzer of Wheaton College if evangelicalism was dying. He said simply, "Absolutely not," and went on to explain, "There's nothing in these data to suggest that Christianity is dying. That Evangelicalism is dying. That Catholicism is dying. That is not the case whatsoever."

Dr. Stetzer asked Smith specifically about what he calls "a cottage industry in Evangelicalism saying the sky is falling." Smith responded,

> With respect to Evangelicalism in particular I would say, that particularly compared with other Christian traditions in the United States, Evangelicalism is quite strong. It's holding its own both in terms of its share of the total population. It's holding its own in terms of the number of Americans who identify with Evangelical Christianity. If you look at Christianity as a whole . . . the share of Protestants in the United States who are Evangelicals is, if anything, growing.[1]

If anything, growing. There are few people who know as much about these things as Greg Smith.

Dr. Stetzer also interviewed Professor Rodney Stark, codirector of Baylor University's Institute for Studies of Religion and the school's distinguished professor of the social sciences. Professor Stark has been at this work much longer than most, and he has grown very impatient with the "sky is falling" falsehood. He is not shy about voicing that impatience, as you will see. Dr. Stetzer asked him about his perspective on the state of evangelicalism in terms of decline. Stark had this to say: "Well, I think this notion that they're shrinking is stupid. And it's fiddling with the data in quite malicious ways. I see no such evidence."[2]

What I have called the Chicken Littles, he playfully called the Bad News Bearers, adding, "[They] make a living coming and saying, 'Church is going to hell . . . everything's going.' . . . And they're always wrong." He also complained that "one of the standard ones just drives me nuts is, 'Young people are leaving the church in droves, what are we going to do?'" He finds no evidence for this, and much to the contrary. We will observe the larger body of research in support of Stark's conclusions on young adults later. It does not tell a Chicken Little story by any stretch.

Smith and Stark are not the only deeply respected scholars and specialists on this topic. As we will see, there are *many* more, and they hail from leading research organizations. Two sociologists working jointly—Sean Bock from Harvard and Landon Schnabel from Indiana University—were recently interested in exploring the apparent reality that faith is declining precipitously in the United States. They wanted to test the assumption that our nation is on a trajectory toward staggering secularization like many parts of Western Europe are experiencing. They call this the "secularization thesis," the idea that modern life, cultural advancement, the abundance of material possessions, and the dominance of a scientific worldview inevitably translate into a culture where religion becomes increasingly irrelevant and relegated to the blue-hair pensioners and a few superstitious, anti-science hangers-on. These two scholars asked whether this was indeed true, and tested this thesis using some sophisticated measures. Their findings? It's certainly not what most would have guessed. Not at all.

What made their study unique was that they measured not only faith practices and beliefs, things like prayer habits, church attendance, and one's view of the authority and trustworthiness of the Bible, but also the *intensity* of faith, the seriousness with which people practiced and believed these things. For instance, they wanted to find out not just whether but how *often* people pray as a general habit. Only when in crisis or only when it comes to mind? Or do they do so daily as a regular part of their lives? How often do they attend church? Are they only Christmas and Easter types, once or twice a month, or the weekly/more than once a week stalwarts? What is their view of Scripture? Do they read and study the Bible as the actual, trustworthy, authoritative Word of God, or do they see it as merely a good book of inspiration?

The gold of their investigation was being able to distinguish what we can call the *dabblers* from the *diligent disciples*. This is important because a major assumption of many is that the more so-called "progressive and enlightened" churches that have changed their beliefs to match the times would be growing. Wanting to keeping current with the modern age, people would certainly migrate toward those congregations that no longer harped on sin and hold that "old idea" of a need for repentance and forgiveness. Surely congregations teaching that miracles are for ages past would hold more attraction to the modern mind, and loosening up on obedience to traditional sexual ethics would be seen as more welcoming and noncondemning. And certainly stringent churches that stress these things would be shrinking, because who wants to hear about all that?

These two scholars' findings were clear and remarkably counterintuitive. In the introduction of their study, they let their readers know point blank:

> We show that rather than religion fading into irrelevance as the secularization thesis would suggest, intense religion—strong affiliation, very frequent practice, literalism and evangelicalism—is *persistent*, and in fact, *only* moderate religion is on the decline in the United States.[3]

Get that. Only moderate religion is on the decline in the US. Their findings show, as they explain, "the United States has demonstrated *sustained levels of intense religiosity* [of which they mean Christianity primarily] across key measures over the past decades that are unique when compared to other advanced, industrial societies."[4] They go so far as to say that the US is a marked exception and distinguished counterexample to the secularization thesis. In the United States, Christian faith that takes Scripture and the spiritual disciplines seriously has remained vibrant over the past few decades, right up to the present day. Lukewarm faith and practice, however, have been on a marked downward trajectory across every measure they examined.

Of course, this conclusion flies directly in the face of the common story line that so many of us have been told time and again from those inside and outside of the church. These scholars do note the rapid rise of those who report they are unaffiliated with any institutional faith today—the infamous and little understood "nones," which we will examine fully and clarify carefully later—a number that has more than doubled since the late 1980s. However, they also find what they describe as "a patently persistent level of strong affiliation" over the past few decades, demonstrating what they call "a very stable trend line."

What this means, of course, is that while the number of people who have a lukewarm faith and who are dabblers is declining significantly—and we will see plenty of evidence for this as we go on— robust, *diligent discipleship* congregations are holding like an anchor with remarkable consistency. In fact, the data show that believers who pray many times a day have increased by more than 8 percent since 1991 and those who attend church services more than once a week rose slightly. Pew Research Center findings show the same thing over the last decade, as we will see shortly. The number of evangelical young adults is also rising, as we shall learn in chapter 7. For those keeping score at home, holding steady and even rising slightly is not declining. That sounds like very good news, but we have not even scratched the surface in our investigation yet.

The Indiana University/Harvard research, in agreement with Pew's Greg Smith, says that "evangelicals are not on the decline" but actually "grew from 1972 when they were 18 percent of the population, to a steady level of about 28 percent from 1989 to 2016." This particular "percentage of the population" measure is very significant, and it's important to clarify its significance. It shows not only growth in terms of real numbers, but enough growth to keep up with or even exceed the rate of population growth. That's not nothing.

Suppose you were working hard to attract and hold a crowd as a business owner, university president, indie music artist, community volunteer coordinator, or banana stand operator. Whatever line of work you were in, you would be absolutely giddy at experiencing this kind of growth, and you'd be right to be. You could call yourself very successful, and it would be difficult to reasonably challenge you on your sense of accomplishment. This the present state of evangelicalism, and it's the opposite of what would animate Chicken Little.

In contrast, the Indiana/Harvard research showed that mainline Protestants[5] have declined precipitously from 35 percent of the American population in 1972 to 12 percent of the population in 2016. *This* is Chicken Little territory. The decline of the mainline churches began in 1960s and early 1970s as they started to question and even officially change their positions on historic Christian basics like the existence of miracles, the reality of sin, and the actual atoning death of Christ and His resurrection, as well jettisoning biblical convictions about sex, gender issues, and abortion. People ran for the doors of these churches in mass with every new compromise, and this exodus continues today. Compromising biblical truths was and is a devastating church-growth strategy. It could hardly be worse if these pastors *asked* their parishioners to leave and never come back.

Because of these changes, the Indiana/Harvard researchers explained that, of people who were affiliated with a church, the only group that increased was those who were more robust and traditional in their beliefs and practices, from 39 percent of all church attenders in 1989 to 47 percent in 2017. Therefore, Christianity in America—and in most other places in the world, as we will see in chapter 6—is growing more vibrant and traditional.

So is Christianity shrinking?

Not if you're talking about the biblically faithful congregations that call their people to genuine Christian discipleship. Only from the mainline churches do you hear that big sucking sound emanating. Most of these congregations are free falling as if they have a millstone tied to their necks. And the more liberal they are, the faster they plummet. People can't get out of these churches fast enough. Though, as we shall see later, there are a few mainline churches that are indeed actually growing.

Let me tell you a story about one of these churches that recently made a deliberate shift away from basic Christian orthodoxy and lost significant membership because of it: EastLake Church in Seattle. It's an interesting case study because this was a fabulously growing church that made dramatic changes in doctrine and practice in a very short period of time and the effects were immediate. It was not a mainline church in any sense. EastLake Church began as your average hipster evangelical church appealing to and connecting with young people. The founding pastor, Ryan Meeks, watched his church explode in the early years, seeing more than one hundred new people come week after week. The mushrooming growth was certainly a struggle, but it was the kind of problem every pastor welcomes, and Meeks was no different. The church continued to grow in terms of people in the seats, volunteers, services, staff, finances, and additional campuses throughout Seattle.

But a few years ago, Meeks made a major theological shift. With great fanfare, he announced one weekend that EastLake would become fully supportive of homosexuality. No, they would not just be kind and gracious to people who identify as same-sex attracted who come through their doors. They were already doing that. All churches should do that. He decided his church would now affirm, even *embrace*, homosexuality itself. In the course of one weekend, they became a pro-LGBT church, with Meeks making stunning statements like, "I don't care if the Bible says, 'Gay people suck.' I have lots of things I disagree with about the Bible."[6] He disparaged the Scriptures in other ways, telling his congregation, "If we need to consult an ancient book to know what to do when a human is standing in front of us, I think we're screwed already." That from a pastor trying to make his church more relevant and welcoming to the people in his city. They changed nothing else but this position and had their pastor's radical statements on the record.

So what happened at EastLake Church after this shift? Did even more people flock in, given their greater openness and acceptance? In an online video from the church, Meeks doesn't mince words. He explains the church imploded. They lost members by the hundreds. Their budget tanked by millions of dollars. They had to lay off much of their staff and close campuses. Ironically, even the lesbian staffer, whose participation in the church and "coming-out" compelled Meeks to make this major change so she would feel more welcome, lost her job. All because their pastor said, "I don't care what the Bible says!" and began making theological decisions that proved it. And it should be noted, that these were not a bunch of reactionary tradition-alists. These were folks very open to innovation and out-of-the box thinking. It's why they were drawn to EastLake.

Ideas and beliefs have consequences. EastLake Church is not a one-off. Not even close. It is only one of thousands of such churches making major theological compromises over the last few decades. Is Christianity shrinking? Some parts of it, you bet. Churches that throw biblical truth overboard find their members jumping overboard after it. The research reveals this, likely as do your observations as you look around your own city.

Is Christianity growing? The better parts of it are. The Indiana/Harvard researchers explained that since the early 1970s, "evangeli-calism rapidly grew and rose to prominence in the public sphere."[7] And that has largely remained so.

Let me close out this examination of this particular study by quoting two strong conclusive statements these authors make about their findings. The first comes early in their article:

> We show that the United States has demonstrated sustained
> levels of intense religiosity across key measures over the last
> few decades that are unique when compared to other advanced
> industrial nations . . . [and] religious change the United States
> is demonstrably different than that in comparable countries
> and that the United States remains an exceptional outlier and
> potential counterexample to the secularization thesis.

Their closing sentence for the article is as direct as it is short: "American religion remains persistently and exceptionally intense."[8] And by religion, they primarily are referring to Christianity.

WHAT ABOUT THE GOOD OL' DAYS?

If you were asked what the most churchgoing age in America was, what would you say? Would you guess the 1950s? Sometime in the 1800s? The colonial times? The answer will surprise you. Professor Rodney Stark, whom we heard from earlier, explains that in 1776, only 17 percent of Americans attended a local church. These were the days when the church steeple was the central landmark of most cities. By 1850, that number mushroomed to 34 percent of Americans, and in 1906, 51 percent attended church. Today, around 69 percent of Americans attend a local church.

Now, let's be clear. This certainly does not mean that 69 percent of Americans are super Christians. Nor were most super Christians back in the day. Many attend church occasionally, but it's important to know that, in line with the Indiana/Harvard research, the "good ol' days" were not way back when, and the heavily secularized days are not today. The number of weekly attenders from all denominations is only 35 percent, and it was 44 percent in the mid-'50s. But it is not cataclysmically worse today compared to any other time in the history of the church, and nearly all of that decline is found in the more liberal churches

The General Social Survey (GSS) is a major and ongoing national research project conducted, gathered, and maintained by the world-class National Opinion Research Center (NORC) at the University of Chicago. Both the GSS and NORC are the gold standard; they are universally respected and are regularly utilized by sociologists of all specialties and perspectives. The GSS has a great deal of data tracking trends in religious practice over the past decades right up to the present. Their data is readily available online, and some of it is relatively easy to access and understand.[9] Their data largely aligns with the Indiana/Harvard research as well as what we will continue to learn through the rest of this chapter and the following ones. Let's take a quick survey of their findings.

Remarkably, the General Social Survey shows that the number of those who attend church more than once a week, such as Sunday service and mid-week Bible study or other small groups, has actually increased slightly overall since 1970. This is the case for each major socioeconomic group, those of all income and educational levels, working classes, races, political affiliations, and regions of the country. That number has also remained generally steady in all age groups—from eighteen to sixty-five and beyond—since 1970 to today. This is absolutely remarkable. We must note that this sort of robust constancy for any behavior across social groupings is extremely rare in the social sciences.

The same trends are true for those who indicated that they prayed more than once a day. The eighteen to thirty-four age range actually saw an increase of a couple percentage points here, while the over-sixty-five group saw a noticeable decline. It is unclear what's behind these curious trends, but the young adults are praying more.

The percentage of people who say they "strongly agree" that they try to carry "their faith belief into everyday life" has remained generally stable between 1970 and today. The percentage of those who "disagree" remained stable as well. Which means there's been very little variation between those who do and those who do not try to live out their faith on a daily basis.[10] These contrasting categories are not losing or gaining practitioners, but staying constant overall.

WHAT DO THE FOLKS AT PEW SAY?

The experts at the Pew Research Center provide us with some of the best and consistently strong and most reliable information on the fuller picture on what's happening with the Christian faith in America. We heard from their associate director of research, Greg Smith, at the beginning of this chapter. Pew describes itself as a "nonpartisan fact tank," tracking the movements in religious practice, belief, and affiliation very reliably. There are few who work in this field of study who don't appraise them highly. They are unarguably the best nonacademic group on this topic, and their findings are extensive.

While they put out numerous reports on various aspects of religiosity each year, their largest and most comprehensive report was released in 2015: *America's Changing Religious Landscape*. Its central finding was that Christians have indeed declined sharply as an overall percentage of the American population, and those unaffiliated with any faith or the nones increased markedly. Specifically, the percentage of adults who describe themselves as Christians in the United States *declined* by a remarkable *eight percentage points* in just seven years, while those who reported they did not identify with any particular religious faith tradition or institution *increased more than six percentage points* over the same time.[11] Disturbing numbers, to be sure.

So what are we to make of these numbers in light of what we have already learned and will continue to learn? What about what we just heard from Pew's own Greg Smith? Is there a conflict? As we will see, these two things—the decline of those who identify as Christians and the rise of the nones—are closely linked in a way that is little understood by most folks today, and their connection is where the real story lies!

Of course, this decline-of-the-church-and-growth-of-the-nones development is what was reported far and wide and has become the established, unquestioned story line. It was generally the only part of the Pew research most mainline media outlets reported on. Their journalists did not seem interested in doing their job of actually reading the report. This finding is largely what's led to the collective "the church is shrinking" hand-wringing from Christians and the "they will soon be gone and out of our hair" hoorays by the more angry atheists and secularists. And these stats, as they stand, are generally accurate. But they are totally misleading if we stop there. The "rest of the story" is very important and changes the whole picture.

Anyone interested in this fuller story must dig into the more granular and essential details to get the larger, more accurate picture. Unfortunately, it was and is the rare mainstream journalist or news outlet that does any such thing. A precious few in the popular Christian press did dig deeper and tell the larger story, but their voices are largely drowned out by the others accepting and repeating the Chicken Little line.

As we continue to closely examine the fuller data of the Pew Research Center, we shall see it all depends on what *kind* of Christianity is shrinking.

Pew's *America's Changing Landscape* states that between 2007 and 2014, mainline Protestant churches declined by 5 million adult members; taking into account margin of error, that number could be as high as 7.3 million lost members. Regardless, the loss is massive.

But here is the part you didn't hear. Churches in Pew's "evangelical" category continued to grow in absolute numbers by about 2 million between 2007 and 2014. Pew explains that with their margin of error, this number could be an *increase* of as many as 5 million evangelical attendees at the highest, or it could have simply remained stable at the lowest. That's not bad news.

Historically black denominations, which are generally more traditional in their theology than the typical mainline congregations, have remained rock-solid stable in members.

As for the Catholics, they declined by 3 million overall. But by Pew's margin of error, it could be a decline of 1 million. Pew reports that, unlike mainline Protestants, "the Catholic share of the population has been relatively stable over the long term, according to a variety of other surveys."[12]

The Catholic church is a peculiarly tricky animal compared to their Protestant brethren when collecting and examining these kinds of numbers. Protestants divide themselves by identity, theological temperaments, and houses of worship with great clarity: the mainlines, and the evangelicals, and nondenominationals. One group goes to church over there, the others go to church over here, and never the twain shall meet. We know who is who.

Catholics are quite different. To be sure, they have very liberal members, very conservative ones, and lots of folks in between. This is true for Catholic clergy as well. What this means is there are lots of Catholics who are similar to liberal Protestants in their approach to Christianity and lots for whom you could refer to as "evangelical" Catholics. Progressives *and* Traditionalists. But here is the trick. Catholics all go by the same name and show up at the same locations on Sunday mornings so it's hard to sort them out.

Unfortunately, polling organizations that provide distinguishable categories for theologically distinct Catholic groups are exceedingly rare. I have not found one. So, like with the Protestants, could liberal Catholics be on the decline and the more conservative holding stable or on the upswing? Or are they the only major Christian group to buck that trend? No one really knows, but it would not be surprising if the same dynamics were at work among our Roman brothers and sisters.

So, Pew is very clear. Christianity is losing members, but nearly all of that loss is among mainline churches. They report that "evangelical Protestants," in contrast to the mainliners, "has remained comparatively stable" as a share of the US population.[13] This "share of the population" measure tells us a more precise story. By Pew's measure, not only has there been actual growth, but there's been enough of an increase to generally keep up with population growth. The distinction is similar to your boss giving you a small percentage annual raise or one indexed to stay ahead of inflation. Both are increases, but one is dramatically more valuable than the other.

In this report, Pew presented a very detailed chart of the growth and decline by Christian denominations as a percentage of the overall US population. The Southern Baptist Convention churches were the only conservative ones that showed a decline between 2007 and 2014. All the other major traditional/evangelical denominations either remained precisely steady or increased just a bit as a percentage of our nation's population.[14] (Quick side note: This same chart showed that those identifying as atheists grew from 2 to 3 percent of the population, and the agnostics—the atheist-lites who are just *not sure* God exists—increased by 2.4 to 4 percent. Yes, a decent increase, but hardly a secularization of America, as the Indiana/Harvard results also demonstrated.)

Pew also explains that evangelicals are the only major Christian group "that has gained more members than it has lost." Read that again. Their folks are not heading for the doors. And the shifts are not just between belief and unbelief, those coming into or exiting the church. It includes those who leave the Episcopal church to join the nondenominational Grace Fellowship over on the east side of town. Pew refers to this as "religious switching," and it is a substantive and dynamic group. So, in terms of people being unhappy with their particular faith tradition, collecting their things, and going elsewhere, evangelicals have benefited more from these ecclesiastical exoduses than anyone else. They even, as we shall see next, outpaced the nones who've been painted as the uncontested winner in the migration game. They are not.

Specifically, Pew reports that nondenominational churches gain roughly five new members for every one it loses to religious switching. Likely most of these are folks leaving the liberalizing mainline swamps for more solid ground rather than leaving the faith or joining the ranks of believers who don't go to church. What is clear is that the nones are *not* coming from the more conservative Protestant churches, and this traffic is not leading toward increased secularization. The Indiana/Harvard research is strongly supported by Pew's findings. We will see just *exactly* where the nones are coming from.

With that, I would like to bring in another important research institute to add to a more precise picture of church switching and the nones: the American Religious Identification Survey (ARIS). Its principle investigator is Professor Barry A. Kosmin, director of the Institute for the Study of Secularism in Society and Culture at Trinity College in Hartford, Connecticut. Kosmin, a sociologist, holds the honor of being able to say to his grandkids, "Did I ever tell you kids about the time I coined the term *nones*? It was all the rage in sociology of religion for a decade or so!" Yep, he's that guy.

While his data shows that the numbers of nones has indeed grown significantly in the last decade, there is another fact he discovered that has not been reported at all, much less really recognized. It concerns the number of Americans who self-reported as nondenominational Christians in contrast to those who newly identified themselves as nones. Dr. Kosmin pointed out an important sub-point to me with some dismay that no one else had picked up on it. He explained, "The rise of nondenominational Christianity is probably one of the strongest [religious growth] trends in the last two decades" in the United

States. He added that the percentage gain is "many times larger" compared to those we have come to know as the nones.[15]

Read that again. *Growth of nondenominational churches has been many times larger than the nones.* Have you ever heard that reported? So it's not the rise of the nones that is the major story of faith growth trends in America, but the long, consistent rise of nondenominational Christianity. And nearly all nondenominational churches are of a more conservative, evangelical flavor, even though they do not identify with a particular denominational tradition. In fact, in many ways, these churches mark the development of a whole new loose denomination of independent churches. You will see them all around your city if you know what to look for.

CONCLUSION

So this is why a yes *and* no answer to our main question of church decline is the correct one. Christianity is shrinking, *and* it is growing. It's just depends on which branch we're talking about. The liberalizing church has been and still is hemorrhaging members as if its carotid arteries have been severed. And they figuratively have, of course, as the church's main supply of life blood is its theology of who Christ actually is, what He has saved us from, and how He did it. If Jesus is not God and sin is not real, then the cross—the center of the Christian story—means nothing. Those leaving these liberal churches in staggering numbers know this all too well. It's why they are going elsewhere.

At the same time, the most vibrant forms of evangelicalism have either remained steady or seen substantial growth. Specifically, it's the evangelical churches identifying as nondenominational that have been growing faster than any others including the nones and the atheists. And as we shall see in chapter 7, young adults are very much involved in the growth of these churches as well.

Pew reports that evangelicals now constitute a clear majority (55 percent) of all US Protestants, and in agreement with ARIS, the share of evangelicals who moved to identifying with a nondenominational church increased from 13 to 19 percent. The Pew report explains, "The family that shows the more significant growth is the nondenominational family."[16] This important addition to the story makes the whole discussion a horse of a very different color than the one that has been shown to most of us. It's very much a good news story and one that needs more telling. It's the "nons" and not the "nones" that are mushrooming.

CHAPTER 3

THE EXPLOSIVE GROWTH
OF "THE NONS"

As we just saw, of all the growth among all the various faith groups, including the infamous nones, research shows us that is it is actually the nondenominational churches that have seen the most explosive growth. There is no doubt about that. And we must also appreciate that it's the very rare nondenominational church that is more liberal. Nearly all are generally faithful in teaching their congregants the traditional truths of Scripture, have meaningful and lively worship derived directly from biblical texts, and call its members to grow weekly in their life in Christ in practical and demonstrable ways and to serve the needs of the community around them. These are the heart of basic Christianity. Increasingly, evangelicalism is being made up of such churches since the early 1980s. They continue to grow, with many of them so large they are referred to as megachurches.

Mega is not an imprecise term. We all know what it means. Many have extremely large buildings and require multiple services on Saturday night and Sunday to serve all the attendees. Many require help from local police officers to direct traffic when their services let out. Others have been required to establish numerous campuses around the city to handle the crowds. Their doors are seldom locked as they have individuals coming in and out from dawn to well past dusk to take advantage of different programs and opportunities.

There is no other age of the church where the growth of so many churches in the United State and throughout the world has been true! Today is that exceptional time. Increasing numbers of such non-denominational churches are getting their starts in school gyms or large rooms at the local Y that host spin and Zumba classes during the week. Some even started in the founding pastor's own living room as a small Bible study and grew from there. You no doubt have seen these populating your city. There's a very good chance you've attended one. In terms of the growth of biblically faithful, spiritually vibrant, disciple-making Christianity, Chicken Little will find very little to squawk about here.

Add to this Pew's finding that the percentage of the US population who describe themselves as "born-again" and/or "evangelical" increased by 1 percent from 2007 to 2014, at the very time the dire Chicken Little warnings were being most fearfully broadcast.[1] One percent is not large, to be sure, but it is growth, particularly when it's tracking ahead of population growth. It's like a business growing 1 percent ahead of inflation. Nothing to party over, but it's not nothing. This is especially significant because the growth occurred at a time when—because we are told so often by the more enlightened in major media—both of these identities had seriously negative public-approval ratings. Apparently an increasing group of people don't feel that way. They are seeking and moving toward a faith that actually is rooted in truth and requires something of them.

Let's now look at some additional research findings from Pew that examine the health of Christian belief and practice from a little different perspective: actual belief and practice.

UPTICK IN THE GOOD DISCIPLINES

As we witness the growth of the nondenominational church it is helpful to also examine what people actually *do* as a part of their faith and whether these are increasing or decreasing. As James, the apostle and brother of Jesus, said, "Faith by itself, if it does not have works, is dead."[2] One's Christianity doesn't really exist if it consists only of belief, as good and correct as that belief might be. Real faith must be demonstrated through spiritual disciplines like studying the Scriptures, prayer, meditation, serving others, and so forth. As the Indiana/Harvard, Pew, and ARIS findings demonstrate, churches that call their members to do these sorts of things in serious ways, the more conservative denominations and nondenominational churches, are being rewarded with people's feet . . . or with the other part of the body they put in the pews or stackable chairs.

It's worth noting that the report from Pew that provides the following data on strong trends on belief and behavior was titled "U.S. Public Becoming Less Religious." It is not surprising then that the headlines spreading across the world would contribute to the "sky is falling" narrative. But most journalists apparently read no further than the title, as the subtitle of the report, appearing right there on the cover, added "but Religiously Affiliated Americans Are as Observant as Before." And despite the apocalyptic title of their report, the folks at Pew state clearly in their introductory executive summary:

> The portion of religiously affiliated adults who say they regularly read scripture, share their faith with others and participate in small prayer groups or scripture study groups all have increased modestly since 2007.[3]

Wow. Read that again and ask yourself if you ever recall seeing such information in any news story in the last ten years. It's certainly not because you've not been paying attention. I've never read it either, nor have any of my colleagues who follow this stuff for a living. In addition, Pew found that those who regularly attend church today are even more likely to rely on the beliefs they learn there, rather than from the larger culture, as their primary guide in determining right from wrong, up at least 7 percent over the last decade. That's a very substantive and growing influence coming from the church. Imagine a local survey in your city that found your neighbors are 7 percent more likely to say they rely on the news from television station X over station Y as their primary guide in making important community decisions. The manager and owner of that station would be justifiably doing some enthusiastic form of the happy dance at such news. So should pastors and their staff.

Let's look at some of the specific ways people are increasingly living out the basics of their Christian lives.

Faith Is Very Important

The percentage of Americans—both Protestant and Catholic—who say their faith is "very important" to them increased two percentage points since 2007, and the percentage of those who say it is not important at all has declined. Like the Indiana/Harvard research, this data seems to indicate a slight increase in Americans who take their faith very seriously, a growth toward a more robust Christianity. There's no bad news in that.

They Pray Daily

Overall, the percentage of American's who identify as Christians and say they pray *daily* beyond a church service increased from 66 to 68 percent from 2007 to 2014. Of US adults who identify as evangelicals, 79 percent say they pray at least once a day, up a smidge from 78 percent in 2007. Those who pray weekly, monthly, or seldom remained level at between 17 and 4 percent. Nothing big to celebrate here necessarily, but God doesn't seem to be increasingly getting the cold shoulder.

They Attend Church More

According to this research, the overall number of Christians who say they attend church weekly fell by only one percentage point since 2007. But the number of evangelicals who say they attend church weekly remained stable over that time. Those who say they attend once or twice a month increased 2 percent. It's not clear if the 1 percent decrease is from established congregants who are attending less, or if the 2 percent increase is due to new folks who are slowly wading into the church with measured attendance frequency.

(Research note: The fact that these numbers on church growth are a bit different from other Pew numbers and those from other institutions demonstrates that due to different ways of examination, different numbers can arise. These are not necessarily contradictory, but merely different views of the same thing seen from different angles. This is common in the social sciences and nothing to necessarily be concerned about. Additionally, numbers can be found that counter those being presented here. The reliable means of overcoming this apparent problem is to examine the larger forest of research instead of individual trees here and there. This is the approach we are taking in these pages.)

They Share Their Faith More Often

Growing numbers of regular church attenders say they share their faith with others, an increase from 24 to 26 percent between 2007 and 2014. These increases were seen among both Protestants and Catholics.

They Read God's Word More Frequently

There are also more US adults reading the Bible at least once a week than there were in 2007. Taking all Christian denominations together, those who read the Bible at least weekly increased a marked 41 to 45 percent from 2007 to 2014. The highest percentage of adults who read their Bible every week are evangelicals, at 63 percent.

On top of this, an academically based think tank at Gordon-Conwell Seminary that tracks faith-trend data reports that the annual demand for Bibles continues to increase notably every year. Thus, more Bibles are printed every year, an increase of about 3 percent annually. This is a notable increase when examined decade by decade. Growth in demand has been true as long as such figures have been collected, and it remains true today. The projections show this will continue well into 2050.[4] Hardly an indication of increasing secularization.

They Have Greater Small Group Participation

The percentage of Americans who say they attend a weekly small group for prayer, Bible study, or any kind of religious education has increased slightly for most denominational categories. The increase among evangelicals grew by three percentage points and among Catholics four percentage points.

This is an incredibly significant measure for the state of spiritual education and development in our nation when we consider three things. *First*, these numbers increased ahead of population growth. *Second*, this growth is for those who attend church *weekly or more*. Super God-squad types. *Third*, a great deal of spiritual development, biblical education, seeing prayer answered in important and even miraculous ways, developing meaningful friendships with like-minded believers, and receiving encouragement in one's faith can all be powerful parts of such small groups. People doing more of these are a very good indicator of church health and spiritual development. It would be hard to see it any other way.

PUBLIC VIEWS OF THE CHURCH

Pew's findings here about how the general public appraises Christians and the church overall are very surprising if you accept the current popular assumptions at face value that Christianity is falling out of favor and needs to rework its public image. As you read each header here, guess what you think the data will say about the population's overall answers.

Do Churches Improve Communities?

Does the general public take a positive or negative view of the church? You will likely be surprised to learn that nearly nine out of ten Americans—whether part of a church or not(!)—*agree* that churches are a wholesale benefit to their cities, that they bring people together and strengthen community bonds, and that they play an essential role in helping the poor and needy. Three-quarters of Americans say churches play a key and positive role in upholding and protecting morality in their communities. This has remained unchanged since about 2010. What community group would not be absolutely giddy with such numbers?

How Do Non-Christians See the Church?

When it comes to the reputation of the church according to non-believers, these findings will surprise nearly everyone as well.

Remarkably, 81 percent of *unaffiliated* Americans (nones, atheists, and agnostics) believe the church serves an important role in bringing people together and strengthening community bonds. Specifically, Pew says that 75 percent of *atheists* in our nation believe this!

Regarding helping the poor and needy, 78 percent of unaffiliated Americans believe the church does an important work here, and 71 percent of atheists specifically feel this way.

When it comes to the church playing a key role in protecting and strengthening community morality, the numbers are lower, but still remarkable. Fifty-four percent of all unaffiliated Americans and 52 percent of agnostics believe the church plays a vital role in preserving moral standards. Thirty-one percent of atheists agree.

This great majority of secularists do not think Christians are just moral busybodies who should stay indoors. Most see their presence and influence in the community as a beneficial and even essential social virtue.

In distinct contrast, only 7 percent of American adults express *mostly* negative views about churches. Only seven percent. Forty-two percent have mostly positive feelings, while 50 percent express mixed feelings. Of those who attend church, 46 percent have mixed feelings about the church.

Of course, this view from within the church looks troubling, but we shouldn't necessarily see these folks as those with a sour disposition toward the church or as moderate whiners. This number could well include many who are absolutely committed to Christ's bride but see concerning problems with its current demonstration in the world. This would include very committed pastors who see more of the church's dirty laundry than the rest of us. So that 46 percent should not necessarily be taken as bad news. Jesus, Paul, and the other disciples had more than mixed feelings toward the church, after all. Look at God's severe judgment of the church in the first chapters of the book of Revelation. The Protestant Reformation was the demonstration of some "mixed feelings" about the church, as is every new denomination that gets launched. Dissatisfaction has a long pedigree in church life.

Regarding actual beliefs about spiritual matters, the findings from this same Pew report are mixed, but certainly not Chicken Little worthy.

What Is Their Belief in Heaven?

While the overall percentage of Americans who believe in heaven has declined slightly, it has increased two or three percentage points among Christian denominations, ranging in the 80s. Curiously, though, while Christians who believe in heaven have increased from 2007 to 2014, among self-identified evangelicals, it climbed to 88 percent. Eighty-eight percent. It begs the question, what in the world does the 12 percent believe about eternal life and the reason Christ died? It could be equally entertaining and distressing to ask them what they believe happens after this life ends and why. Reincarnation? Permanent purgatory? An eternal nap? Never-ending shopping trip to the angel mall? This is clearly evidence that all is not peachy in the church in terms of theological understanding, to be sure. It is cause for concern, but not for a freak-out.

How do They View the Word of God?

Pew shows that the great majority of Christians of all denominations today believe the Bible to be the actual, reliable Word of God. This increased 2 percent since 2007 to 75 percent. For evangelicals, 88 percent, nearly nine in ten, believe this, with no increase or decline since 2007. While we would certainly wish for more conviction in this area, it is no cause for a freak-out either.

There's a very important aspect of this general research question that's worth paying attention to as you read other polls on this topic, or even respond to such polls yourself. Nearly all polls usually ask if the respondent believes the Bible should be taken "literally" or "not literally." Even serious Christian pollsters ask this.

How would you answer? Think carefully. If I were to be true to the question, I would have to laugh and respond, "No, I certainly do not take the Bible literally and *nobody* should." Am I a mushy-headed heretic? Not at all. I know there are many parts of the Bible that should not be taken literally . . . and so do you. Only those who've lost touch with reality believe all the Bible is *literally* true. Let me clarify this essential distinction.

If the question were, "Do you believe the Bible is true, trustworthy, and authoritative in all that it says?" I would give a resounding yes, and I hope you would too. So what's the difference? Before we get into the distinctions, it's important to note that a serious and faithful view of Scripture demands we know and help others understand this difference.

We must take a really commonsense view of the various parts that make up the whole of Scripture. Is it all to be taken literally? Some parts are to be taken literally and others certainly not. Consider Jesus's own sayings. He told us, "I am the way, and the truth, and the life."[5] Is He to be taken literally? Indeed, He *literally is* the Way, the Truth, and Life, for this is precisely who Christ is and why He came. When Jesus said He would be killed and rise again on the third day,[6] was He speaking literally? Of course, for that is precisely what happened on an actual, historic day almost two thousand years ago in Jerusalem, and it serves as the center of our faith. That wonderful event is what Easter is about and makes Christianity completely unique.

Let's look at what Jesus says about Himself from another angle. In the gospel of John chapter 10, Jesus said a number of interesting things about Himself that every faithful Christian takes as positively true. He tells us, "I am the door of the sheep." Later in the chapter He says, "I am the door. If anyone enters by me, he will be saved and will go in and out and find pasture." Both are true, but are they *literally* true? All reasonable people know He is speaking metaphorically. If Jesus is literally a door or the sheep's gate, it would be totally reasonable to ask what side His hinges are on. Does He open automatically of His own power or does the Father open Him? What kind of handle does He have? Is He painted, and if so, what color? What kind of pasture is this we are supposed to find when we do pass through Him?

If these questions seem disrespectful about our Lord, that is the very point. It is ridiculous to ask such questions because we all know He is not literally a door. It is, however, wholly reasonable to ask specific questions about His literal humanness. How tall was He? What was His skin color? What was the texture of His hair? What did His face look and His voice sound like? Why? Because Jesus was literally and truly a real flesh and blood man while also being God. He was not literally a door.

We know there is much of the Bible, especially in the Psalms and Proverbs, that is true and reliable, but beautifully figurative. Thus, when polling questions ask if the Bible should be taken literally, we would hope no one would answer yes. It is deeply unfortunate that the "literal" question is a mistaken effort to determine whether the respondent believes the Bible is a total, reliable authority, especially when answered that way by people who claim to be more serious students of Scripture. No good student should tolerate such a profoundly incorrect assumption about their beloved text. And scholars studying this question should know better. We should immediately correct any such misunderstanding.

Should Christianity Get with the Times?

This is an important question. Those outside the faith often ask, "When are you Christians going to get with the times and realize that . . . ?" and any number of things are suggested that the church should get a clue about: miracles, sin, the devil, abortion, the origins of the world, free sex, homosexuality, overpopulation, et cetera. Wouldn't it be great if Christianity would just get out of the Dark Ages and step into the happy and informed light of modernity?

Well, if you ask this of those in the pews, across the board they are more likely to say the church *should* preserve its traditional beliefs rather than trade them for new fashionable, modern ones or even merely make adjustments. This is why they are leaving the churches that have accommodated. For evangelicals, those who believe the church should preserve traditional beliefs and teachings increased 2 percent from 2007 to 2014 and those who said adjusting certain traditions in light of new circumstances would be okay showed no increase. Those who said the church should adopt "more modern views" increased by 1 percent. Evangelicals who responded "don't know" declined by 3 percent. Any way you look at it, our pews are certainly not calling out for a revolution in more modernist thinking.

Are There Many Roads to Heaven?

We often hear it said that many roads lead to heaven, just as long as people are sincere about their beliefs. When some guest on *Oprah* or a late-night talk show says that, the audience launches into immediate applause. These people don't think it matters if someone holds a particular religious belief. Abraham for the Jews, Jesus for us Christians, and Mohammed for the Muslims become merely characters in a story if they all lead to the same place in the same way. The specifics of any one faith are essentially window dressing, suitable to one's own tastes.

There is both good and bad news here according the Pew data. Overall, the percentage of Christians who believe all roads lead to heaven has decreased slightly since 2007 and has done so in nearly all denominational categories, including the mainliners. It neither increased nor declined for Catholic respondents. It declined the steepest for evangelicals, by five percentage points. That's movement in the right direction.

The bad news is that the belief that all roads leads to heaven sits at a troublingly high level. A very slight majority of evangelicals today say they believe many religions can lead to eternal life. That is very troubling, meaning that a worrisome amount don't take Jesus *literally* when He told us He was *the* Way, *the* Truth, and *the* Life and that no one could come to the Father but through Him. These folks need to get a clue. But test this against how many of your evangelical friends—newbies or mature—actually believe this. Ask around and see if this true in your circles. I doubt you will find a small handful, if any, who hold to this belief, regardless of spiritual maturity. And if you do find any, it will be a helpful opportunity to explain to them the truth.

How Can We Tell Right from Wrong?

The question of how one arrives at what is absolutely right and wrong is a contentious question today. Does right and wrong even exist? In interesting ways, there is growing evidence that absolute relativism is declining today. How do I know? Ask any relativists if they think the election of Donald Trump was absolutely wrong. It is remarkable how clearly and quickly such folks began believing in absolute, nondebatable truth. It is unlikely they will respond by saying Trump supporters have their truth that is just as valid as anyone else's truth. Am I not right?

How many of them would say it's absolutely wrong for a Christian baker, florist, or photographer to refuse to serve a same-sex wedding? What about denying climate change? How many would say it's absolutely *right* to prevent a conservative speaker from speaking on their college campus? Moral outrage is certainly back, even though often misguided. The Left has become the new moral majority, making sure everyone sees things exactly the way they do, or else. The primary problem today is with *how* we arrive at our convictions of what's right and wrong.

Pew wanted to find out what Christians across the board believe about how we should make moral decisions. Where do you think people landed in believing whether one's religion or one's common sense should guide them in determining right from wrong? Not many of us would put our money on religion growing as the primary guide and common sense being seen as less reliable, right?

Remarkably, in all Christian traditions, more people said they relied on their faith than they did in 2007 and *fewer* said they relied on common sense. The shifts over the years for both categories were substantial, even among the mainliners. Those in each denominational category who said philosophy or science was their main guide did increase, but comparatively very slightly and at relatively low levels.

How Important Is Sharing One's Faith?

Of course, a vital part of living out one's faith is the desire to actually share it with others. People who *really* believe what they believe is true and support what their church offers in terms of truth, salvation, and spiritual development are more likely to share that faith with others. People tend to share good news, whatever it might be, with others. It's human nature. Pew's data shows that the percentage of American Christians who share their faith weekly or more has risen since 2007, and it has done so among all major Christian traditions, including mainliners and Catholics. That is a very good sign.

Not surprising, but equally notable, is that atheists, agnostics, and the nones are *less* likely to share their *unbelief* with others. Mormons are the group showing the greatest increase in sharing their faith since 2007, with nearly a 10 percent increase. But among Christian groups, members of the evangelical and historically black churches are most likely to share their faith at least once a week or more, 35 and 44 percent respectively.

What's more, younger evangelicals are more likely to share their faith than those older than sixty-five years of age. And young people have never been inclined to share religious beliefs with their friends unless they feel very strongly they are true. That is likely more true today.

Who Is Feeling Spiritual Peace?

The overall percentage of Americans who say they experience feelings of spiritual peace or well-being at least once a week has grown markedly from a margin of seven to ten percentage points. The increase was greatest among Catholics and lowest among evangelicals.

More Are Thinking about the Meaning of Life

Similarly, the number of those who spend serious time thinking about the meaning of life has increased markedly over the last decade as well, anywhere from five to twelve percentage points. People who are increasingly thinking about questions of ultimate meaning are those who are open to hearing the truth, thus creating greater opportunities for real evangelism. This, and more people sharing the Christian faith as we just saw, creates a very opportune juncture for the church. It seems as if people might increasingly have ears to hear.

Curiously, Pew found that the *greatest* increase in Americans who are pondering the purpose and meaning of life are the atheists who tell us there is no real purpose to life other than what we bring to it. You're born, you live, you die, and then you become food for worms. A seventeen percentage point increase in atheists who are asking the deeper questions of life indicates they have nagging doubts about what they think is true. This should not surprise at all and they might be our community's greatest seekers.

*   *   *

This larger body of the best research on what's happening with Christianity in terms of growth trends in the United States today consistently leaves us with three main takeaways. First, the evangelical nondenominational churches are largely experiencing healthy growth, some moderately and others remarkably so. Any local economy and its business people would be euphoric if it experienced such growth. Second, liberal mainline churches are the ones hurting, and they are hurting badly. Really, as we shall see in chapter 5, their days are numbered. Their ministry model is clearly unsustainable, and what's so troubling is they know it. The numbers are so staggering that no one can miss them. But they continue to dig their own grave. Third, attitudes of those outside of the church toward the social significance of the Christian church, even among atheists, agnostics and nones, remains largely very positive. Atheists are more likely today to be asking the bigger questions about life's meaning.

Many of the most important beliefs and practices among Christians are holding steady and some important ones have increased in the last few years.

As we have now seen about the tremendous growth of *nons* who have no close competitor in religious growth, let us take a close examination of who the *nones* actually are and are not.

CHAPTER 4
THE NONES ARE NOT NEW

The infamous and perplexing nones. They have gotten such a great deal of press in the last ten years, and every pastor knows the term and how it has been defined. You've probably heard your pastor talk about them from the pulpit. However, there's far more confusion than clarity about the nones floating around out there. Actually very few people have a true and correct understanding of them. But a clear and consistent explanation of who they are *does* exist among those who study these things more closely. Christians need to have a correct picture of who these people are and to date, we have not. Let me put it directly:

> The rise in these much talked about and fretted-over nones
> are not people leaving their faith or the church. They are not
> a new kind of unbeliever. They are not actually a new group
> at all. These are folks who are simply being more honest and

accurate in their description of where they have always been in terms of their belief and practice.

This is who the nones are. Their rise is not because of some great secularizing upheaval in American's faith beliefs and practices. They are simply reporting their actual faith practices in more candid ways, largely due to new ways in which polling questions have been asked in the last ten years or so. Dr. Ed Stetzer, a friend who holds the distinguished Billy Graham Chair of Church, Missions, and Evangelism at Wheaton College, has given one of the best clarifying explanations of this phenomenon that I've seen. In *USA Today*, he wrote that "Christianity isn't collapsing, it's being clarified." He is precisely right. He further explains, "Nominal Christians are becoming the nones and convictional Christians remain committed."[1] This is the precise secret to understanding what's going on.

These nominals becoming the nones as Stetzer puts it are simply those who until recently would have identified with a Christian denomination just because that's what their family has always been. But their pastors have only had the joy of maybe seeing them at Christmas, Easter, and funerals. Beyond that, crickets. Thus, these nominal Christians are simply being more honest about what they believe and have long been: *nothing really*. Thus, the "nones." They are not a new kind of unbeliever. Even though they are inactive, many of them do hold some cold to lukewarm Christian beliefs in the back of their minds. So the nones are not some new and growing crowd of the disinterested. Not at all.

Stetzer has very good company in this conclusion. Pew reported in *America's Changing Religious Landscape* that the way they questioned respondents could "make it easier for marginally religious people who once thought of themselves as Catholics, Protestants, or members of another religious group to identify as religious 'nones.'"[2] Rodney Stark of Baylor University, one of the world's leading and distinguished scholars in this field, gives the same explanation in his important book *The Triumph of Faith: Why the World Is More Religious Than Ever*: "Today, when asked their religious preference, instead of saying Methodist or Catholic, now a larger proportion of non-attenders say 'none,' by which they most seem to mean 'no actual membership.'" Stark is saying the nones are simply those who are dropping the pretense of being a part of a church they never really attended in the first place. Stark gets more clear and precise: "*The entire change* [toward none-ness] *has taken place with the nonattending group.*" "In other words," he adds, "this change marks a decrease only in nominal affiliation, not an increase in irreligion." In agreement with the Indiana University/Harvard study we examined earlier, Stark says the wealth of data he has studied "does not support claims for increased secularization, let alone a decrease in the number of Christians. It may not even reflect an increase in those who say they are 'nones.'"[3]

The Indiana/Harvard researchers' explanation of the nones aligns with Stetzer and Stark. They say that any increase in an apparent secularization in America—as evidenced by the growth of the nones—is "solely a function of the decline of moderate religion."[4]

In fact, a 2009 Pew Forum on Religion & Public Life report concluded that only 12 percent of former Protestants and Catholics who have completely walked away from their faith and now counted among the nones had any kind of childhood faith that could be taken as meaningful.[5] Nearly all the nones who have incorrectly been described as bailing on their faith never really had any kind of faith at all. Of course, it's impossible to hang on to what you never really had in the first place.

In contrast, nearly 90 percent of kids coming from homes where they were taught a serious faith retain that faith into adulthood. Read that sentence again. Nearly all kids who grow up in a home that practices and teaches them some sort of vibrant Christian belief and practice retain that faith into adulthood. We will examine why and how this is true in much greater detail in chapter 8. Again, not something the cottage industry Chicken Littles are likely to pay attention to, but it's true.

Thus, we must gain a strong hold of this fact: the rise of the nones is not a new group in the landscape of religion in the United States. They are not a sign of an increasingly secular society losing interest and trust in spiritual matters. This bears repeating: *They are not a sign of an increasingly secular society losing interest and trust in spiritual matters.* The words on the sign under which they have long stood have simply changed from "Don't Really Attend" to "No Affiliation." The nones are merely standing where they've always stood, and it's not in church.

So that is the meat of the story here. Yes, some Christians are leaving the church. Yes, some churches are shrinking, and yes, "none" is a growing identity. But if this is the only story that's being told, it's a false one, even though these three things are factually true in and of themselves. The rest of the story needs to be explained, and this is what has been missing in the larger public conversation. Recall what Professor Kosmin of the American Religious Identification Survey (ARIS) explained to us earlier. He stated, "The rise of nondenominational Christianity is probably one of the strongest [religious growth] trends in the last two decades" in the United States, adding the percentage gain there is "many times larger" compared to those we have come to know as the nones.[6] This fact itself is the very center of the larger story on church growth and decline in our society today.

What is more, young adults are very much a part of this growth, as we will see in greater detail in chapter 7. There simply is no real evidence that secularism is increasing in the United States or that faithful, biblical Christianity is collapsing. Quite the opposite actually. And this truth should be more widely understood and appreciated among the clergy, their staff, those teaching small groups, and those leading others in their faith. The correct demonstrations of faith are growing, and the false ones are shriveling. How can that not be taken as anything but good news?

CHAPTER 5

STICK A FORK IN IT: THE MAJOR FAIL OF LIBERAL CHRISTIANITY

The liberal project in the Christian church, the effort to essentially bail on every important and animating truth of the Christian faith, has a long and checkered past. It didn't start in the 1960s or '70s, as we might think, but in the late 1800s and early 1900s and grew in influence from there. Those liberalizing the church intended to "save" Christianity and its respectability in the modern, scientific era by doing away completely with its miraculous and supernatural aspects. A man who walked the earth couldn't possibly actually be God, but merely pointed us to God, if He even existed at all. That man's greatest miracle was not raising anyone from the dead but raising each of us in our own self-actualization and enlightenment. Jesus never actually did things like multiply the fish and loaves. His teachings of peace, love, and understanding caused others to emulate the sacrificial giving of the young boy who gave his meager lunch. The crowd all came up with their own food for themselves and shared it with others. Everything seemingly divine about Jesus has a wholly reasonable, naturalistic explanation.

The liberalizing churches have embraced abortion with great passion, are ordaining clergy and their same-sex relationships, and perform gay weddings with glee. And they have long tried to teach us that we know better today than to believe sin is actually real and that Christ's death on the cross actually did anything about it. One of my professors in grad school, a very old liberal scholar, would regularly and bitterly denounce what "those silly evangelicals" believed about the wonder working power of the blood of Christ as "butcher shop theology." I remember thinking, as I sat in his class, that Dr. Mountcastle and his sort would have absolutely nothing of meaning or hope to tell anyone dealing with the death of a loved one or the unraveling of life.

So how has the liberal project actually fared? What is its track record? The facts speak as clearly as they do loudly. Time has tested the liberalizing project and judged it harshly. Nearly *all* the decline in Christian identity and church attendance is in the more liberal mainline denominations. This fact puts the whole story into perspective. It is not and has seldom drawn people to itself. People are exiting these churches as if someone pulled the fire alarm. But this is no drill.

The lesson from the liberal's campaign is obvious and simple: *No one goes to church to get watered-down, reconstituted Christianity.*

People don't want churches that reject the basic truths that make Christianity what it is. People who take the trouble to regularly attend church want whole milk, not skim or even 2 percent. Thus, when the mainline churches make their moves toward being more "enlightened and relevant" to the current age, their congregations respond with their feet and do so decisively. We saw this in the example of Seattle's EastLake Church, and it happened with great efficiency, within the course of one or two weeks. The church market responds very quickly to such changes.

A very interesting and starkly counterintuitive example of how even very unlikely people prefer more conservative churches comes from research conducted jointly at Columbia University and UCLA. Examining the church choices of same-sex-attracted men and women, these two scholars found that these individuals were 2.5 times more likely to attend churches that took a more conservative view on homosexuality—churches that these scholars derisively called "non-affirming"—over those congregations that celebrated homosexuality.[1] Pew's findings also show that same-sex-identified individuals are more likely to attend churches that hold to a biblical view of sexuality.[2] Very interesting.

The authors of the Columbia/UCLA study, who are well-established as being advocates for homosexuality, were deeply per-plexed as to why the same-sex attracted would choose churches that they described as having a "hostile social environment to LGB individuals." Well, maybe same-sex-attracted individuals find such churches are indeed *not* hostile. Those "welcoming" rainbow flags you see flying outside a few rare churches are not appealing to the very people they are intended to attract. It's the churches that so many on the left mistakenly and irresponsibly accuse of "hating the gays" that actually care for and accept them as people.

Even the same-sex attracted who make time to go to church seem to want a church that is faithful to what Christianity actually *is*. It's the very rare seeker who searches for Christianity-lite. They want the real thing, not in spite of it making real demands upon them, but very likely *because* of it.

The attractiveness of more faithful church practice, teaching, and approach is demonstrated in another interesting study. A group of sociologists in Canada wanted to investigate if there were any distinct differences between mainline churches that were growing and those that were shrinking and what those might be. They wanted to test a finding that two well-respected scholars in sociology of religion, Roger Finke and Rodney Stark, reported in their classic book *The Churching of America, 1776–2005*.[3] Finke and Stark discovered that, going back deep into the history of our nation, the most significant dividing line between growing and declining churches was their theology. Churches that were more conservative in their theology and practice tended to grow, while those with more liberal beliefs did not do so in the long run, even within the same denomination.

Finke and Stark believed this was true for a number of reasons, all of them practical. Churches with more conservative theology tended to take evangelism and the issue of salvation, deliverance from sin, and growing in Christ more seriously, thus their members were more creative and driven in reaching those outside their walls. They tended to develop more dynamic programs for children and teens in the last one hundred or so years for the very same reasons. Their worship has also tended to be more enthusiastic, vibrant, and contagious because they believed God had *truly* forgiven their *real* sins, had given them *actual* new life, would welcome them into a *real* heaven, and *truly* oversees their daily care until that day comes. This was true in the old days of classic hymns and church organs up to today with choruses and loud, multi-instrumented worship bands. Conservative beliefs and teaching animated worship in practical ways that liberal theology did not and never really has. It's kind of a waste of time to worship a God that is not really God.

In testing Finke and Stark's findings, what did the Canadian researchers discover? Well, let me give you the spoiler. They titled their published study "Theology Matters" because of the clarity of their findings. Comparing and contrasting mainline churches that were growing or shrinking, their data showed conclusively that churches that held more conservative theological beliefs and practices were the ones seeing congregational and spiritual growth. The theologically liberal churches only saw decline. They explained that the theological and spiritual conservatism of the pastor had "a much larger effect" on church growth than the conservatism of the congregants themselves. As goes the pastor, so goes the church. The sheep follow the shepherd, at least when he's taking them to more biblically faithful pastures. Let me show you just three of the dramatic differences in belief between the growing and declining mainline churches.

When pastors were asked if they agreed that "believing Christians have access to real, supernatural power in this life that is not available to nonbelievers," 77 percent of pastors from the growing mainline churches either somewhat or strongly agreed that they do. However, *zero percent* (that's 0.00000!) of declining mainline pastors strongly agreed with that statement, and only 19 percent *moderately* agreed. Most of them thought that statement was largely false. Curious isn't it? People are less likely to attend churches where pastors don't think Christianity has anything really special about it. It's as constant as the law of gravity.

In terms of whether Jesus actually rose from the grave in a real flesh and blood body, ZERO pastors from the growing churches said he most certainly did not. From the declining churches? Nineteen percent of those pastors said he did not. Only 38 percent believe he absolutely did!

Get this, and it might just be a part of the problem. Zero pastors of the declining churches strongly agreed that it was important to encourage non-Christians to become Christians while 77 percent of those from growing churches did. Goodness. How many people do you think want to beat a path to a church that believes their own core message is not worth sharing? Going to brunch instead would be more uplifting. The gaping chasms between the growing and dying mainline churches on fundamentals of Christianity were this stark in nearly all of the categories these scholars examined. Some, more so! Theology matters, indeed.

In addition, both pastors and the people in the pews of growing churches were vastly more likely to say their church put an emphasis on evangelism and overall had a clear mission and purpose for their church's existence. They knew what they were about and it animated the life of their congregation in their community. People are drawn to what is real, authentic, and life changing.

But theology was not the only thing that differentiated the dying from the growing churches. Researchers also found that growing churches put a great deal of emphasis on their youth programs and had more contemporary styles of worship. They were more likely to utilize visual technology such as the projection of song lyrics and video clips for announcements and sermons illustration in their services. Drums, guitars, keyboards, and other instruments were a large part of their worship. They discovered growing churches tended to have younger congregants and younger pastors and staff, and their members put more emphasis on Bible reading, study, small groups, and community evangelism. These Canadian scholars noted that the growing mainline churches "bear a striking resemblance" to the non-denominational churches that are and have been enjoying substantial growth. This was no mere coincidence.

So this is a very significant and interesting finding. It's not just the "mainline-ness" of a church that is associated with decline, but their theology itself. When mainline churches put their emphasis on holding fast to biblical orthodoxy and morals, teaching their young people well, and having engaging, vibrant worship the opposite happens. Theology drives the day. EastLake Church in Seattle, which we looked at earlier as an example of a church whose growth plummeted after rejecting traditional evangelical theology, certainly continues to have engaging worship and innovative use of technology. They continue to offer creative children's and youth programs. But their dramatic compromise on theology was their death knell.

The Canadian scholars are frank in their conclusion that it is abundantly "clear that theological conservatism plays a role in distinguishing growing from declining mainline Protestant churches."[4] These academics would certainly tell Chicken Little she had nothing to squawk about . . . unless she were an agent for the liberal project.

So, we have seen that the greatest movement of growth within Christianity is found among the evangelical nondenominational churches. The nones are not a new or growing category, but merely a change in identity. And the greatest movement in decline within Christianity over the last fifty years, right up to today, is liberal Christianity. It has been a spectacular failure and that fact would be difficult to overstate. The evidence for this is overwhelming and too dramatic to ignore. The precipitous decline of churches preaching watered-down Christianity has been happening long enough and severely enough that it must be seen as a millstone around the neck of those trying to change traditional church doctrine into a wholly neutered and thus other faith. That project's leaders would be wise to admit the unavoidable and go into another line of work or make up a new name for what they have been creating. It's certainly not Christianity.

Actually, there is a name for what these people believe. It's called Unitarianism, and the folks there would be most happy to have the company. They certainly have the room as their congregations are growing sparse as well. The past, present, and future of the church are with the scripturally faithful and spiritually serious. That has been shown here, and it will be in the next chapter as well when we examine what it happening with Christianity around the world.

Let's conclude with this very important observation from recent history. What we are seeing today, this shrinking and growing of different churches and the debate over them, is by no means a recent development. As the writer of Ecclesiastes teaches us, "There is nothing new under the sun."[5] Our age today is not so unique, nor the situation so dire.

In the study of sociology of religion, a classic text is Dean M. Kelley's *Why Conservative Churches Are Growing*. Kelley was one of the top leaders in the liberal National Council of Churches (NCC) back in the day, and he released his book in 1972. It did not win him many friends among his liberalizing peers in or outside the NCC. He started his book with this disturbing warning, which sounds exactly like the cries being broadcast today in so many circles: "For the first time in the nation's history most of the major church groups stopped growing and began to shrink." He added, "Most of these denominations had been growing uninterruptedly since colonial times. . . . Now they have begun to diminish, reversing a trend of two centuries."

Kelley went on to quote a leading expert on church growth from that day who said then precisely what we've learned is going on today. Through the 1960s and into the '70s, this expert observed that "the fundamentalists and Pentecostals increased their numbers at about the same rate as the mainline churches' decrease." Wow. One's growth was the same size as the other's decline. Kelley regrettably agreed, having had great hope for the liberalizing project of the NCC in the Christian church. He lamented, "By this important index of spiritual vitality, the mainline churches are weakening while the rapidly growing [conservative] churches are becoming stronger." Nothing new under the sun indeed.

Dr. Kelley seemed to hyperventilate as he speculated as to why the conservative churches were growing. Like the scholars we noted earlier from Columbia University and UCLA who couldn't for the life of them understand why same-sex-attracted individuals would choose to attend "backward" churches that took a traditional view of human sexuality, Dr. Kelley was dumbfounded by his research results.

With unbounded arrogance, he noted for his readers that these growing churches were "not 'reasonable,' they are not 'tolerant,' they are not ecumenical, they are not 'relevant.' Quite the contrary!" So how in the world could they be growing? he asked. Don't these Christians know what's good for them? He speaks for many of the more "progressive" church men (and women) today when he said, "It is ironic that the religious groups which persist in such 'unreasonable' and 'unsociable' behavior should be flourishing" while the reasonable and sociable were not. Wrestling even more with this conundrum, Kelley seemed almost ready to accept the unacceptable: "It is not only ironic, but it suggests that our understanding of what causes a religious group to flourish is inadequate. Some dynamic seems to be at work which contradicts prevailing expectations."[6]

Some dynamic *seems* to be at work . . . Uhm, what could that possibly be? Perhaps people are drawn to seek truth that is rooted in a faithful teaching and practice of God's Holy Word, one that makes real demands of them and offers genuine change and real hope. Could that dynamic also possibly be the Holy Spirit? Hmm.

His liberal and so-called progressive peers today are scratching their heads over the same thing. For being so well-educated, they are not very good students of history. The truth is precisely what we saw first in the Indiana/Harvard study, right across all those stepping-stones we walked upon right up to the Canadian study here. People have long voted for theological fidelity and its natural companion, spiritual vibrancy. And they continue to do so today in expanding numbers. They would rather take Jesus for who He clearly is in Scripture rather than a "new and improved" modernized fabrication created by the do-gooders who feel Jesus could really benefit from a new public relations director. Their failed project is responsible for the largest and longest collapse in the church in recent history, possibly ever, and they should be forced to own it.

Not only do we know this in our gut and everyday observations, but a wealth of scientific research, which the "reasonable" liberals claim to be all about, is unavoidably clear on the point. It's time to stick a fork in the liberalizing project. It's done, dead, over. One of that movement's most influential contemporary voices is John Shelby Spong who wrote a book some twenty years ago he titled *Why Christianity Must Change or Die*. One wonders if he appreciates the irony there. Experience has indeed shown us he was absolutely correct. He was just tragically wrong about what part of the church needed to change or die.

CHAPTER 6

HOW IS CHRISTIANITY DOING GLOBALLY?

I f you were asked, "What is happening with Christianity around the world? Is it growing or declining?" how would you answer? What is your gut feeling given what you hear from news stories, church leaders, and your own sense of things? How sure would you be about your answer? Do you have any idea about the state of Christianity globally? Many don't.

These are important questions for every Christian to ask, as well as for those outside the faith who simply want to know what's happening with significant global trends. Knowing the movements among leading religions is as critical as following the global trends in economics, education, health care, and politics because religion is as vital to the lives of individuals at the social dynamics of a nation.

Religion is far more than just a private thing people do apart from all the other aspects of their life. What people believe about God, the nature of that belief, how it shapes their lives and their lives with others, and how they live it out is paramount. What world faiths are growing, which are declining, which are evolving, and how? These should be questions of interest to all who claim to be even moderately educated about what's happening in the world.

Of course, the answers to these questions are also of utmost importance to all Christians, as we should all be deeply committed to the health and well-being of the church—our Lord's beloved bride, for whom He died and gave His all—as well as the salvation of the world. Three of the four gospels conclude with Christ's command to take His good news to every nation.

Imagine a person who says he or she is all in and deeply committed to the mission and success of the multinational company he or she works for. They've pledged their total allegiance to its founder and his mission. They show up to work each day, even volunteer extra hours of their lives and conduct themselves totally in line with the corporate culture. They attend all the important meetings, make valuable contributions to the company, and regularly talk up the mission of the organization to their friends and neighbors. Their own personal identity and the company's mission are hard to separate. But . . . they have little to no understanding of what's happening with the services and products of the company worldwide. Where is the growth? Where are the declines? Where are the struggles? The future opportunities? What is driving these? How are the various international offices accomplishing the work? Could we say such a person is really in line with their professed commitment to the company?

All of us as Christians can learn from this comparison. Jesus's last words to all of us were to take the new life He offers to all nations and all corners of the earth. It's the last thing our boss really wanted us to get and not forget. So we should indeed understand how that work is going across the globe.

So, back to our opening questions.

1. How is the Christian church doing worldwide?
2. Is it declining or growing?

This chapter gives us well-rounded answers. But let me give you a quick peek behind the curtain in one sentence: *the story is largely very good news and by most measures, extremely so.* It's a story all Christians should know, celebrate, and contribute to.

One of the most noted and widely respected scholars doing work in the field of tracking the movements of global Christianity is Professor Philip Jenkins of Baylor University, codirector of their program on Historical Studies of Religion in the Institute for Studies of Religion. He also has a dual appointment as the distinguished professor of History and Religious Studies at Penn State University. He has written fourteen academic books on various aspects of religion and multiple more professional journal articles in this field. As the practical dean in this school of global study, we will consult with Professor Jenkins first.

His first book on this topic was *The Next Christendom: The Coming of Global Christianity*. It was highly acclaimed and He followed it up with *The New Faces of Christianity: Believing the Bible in the Global*

South. Professor Jenkins says there are three driving truths anyone must appreciate if they are going to understand the global picture of what *is* and *is not* presently happening or going to happen with Christianity in the remainder of the twenty-first century.

1. Of all the major faiths across the globe, Christianity will leave the deepest mark on the twenty-first century.

In terms of sheer numbers, Christianity is flowering around the world and doing so soundly, even *dominantly*. It exceeds Islam in terms of real numbers by a notable margin and is likely to continue to do so for quite some time. Jenkins told the *Atlantic* in an interview about *The Next Christendom* that "as far as we can see from the numbers right now, Christianity is going to continue to be the world's most numerous religion, as least until the end of the twenty-first century." Specifically, the coming two decades will see the world's population of Christians grow from today's 2 billion to a remarkable 3 billion adherents, making Christianity the world's largest faith for at least the next eighty years.

Jenkins adds in the *Atlantic* article that this will have real consequences for nations as well as for the Christian faith itself. "So if we're looking at the religion that is going to affect the largest number of lives in the twenty-first century, it is almost certainly going to be Christianity."[1] Historian Alvin Schmidt and others have noted that as Christianity has spread across the world through history, it's had an extremely positive and humanizing impact on well-being and human rights.[2] In fact, the very ideal of universal human rights comes from the Christian view of the human person, as it holds that there is no one more or less valuable than another, regardless of race, education, capability, bank account, gender, age, born or unborn. Thus, there is great empirical evidence that the continued and robust spread of Christianity around the world will have deeply positive, practical consequences for the well-being of men, women, and children, and their communities and nations.

Jenkins recognizes the important and desirable influence Christianity has upon the peoples who are increasingly embracing it. "For the growing churches [around the world], the Bible speaks to everyday, real-world issues of poverty and debt, famine and urban crisis, racial and gender oppression, state brutality and persecution."[3] It is improving lives because of what it teaches and demands of people. Christianity is certainly not "pie in the sky" but is life-saving and life-giving, here, today, in the real world.

In his interview with the *Atlantic*, Jenkins laments that while the growth of Christianity globally is a bare and incontestable fact, people in the West just don't seem to get it. The hopefulness of what is actually happening on the ground in most countries is in direct contradiction to the more popularly held assumption that the church is dying. "For more than a century," he explains in his book *The Next Christendom*, "the coming decline or disappearance of religion has been a commonplace assumption of Western thought, and church leaders have sometimes shared this pessimistic view."[4] Much of this is and has been couched in the language that the Christian church must get out of the past and join the future; it must ditch its old, dusty ideas on miracles, sin, the blood sacrifice of God's own Son, and particularly on the issues of sexuality, or it will shrivel up and die.[5] As we saw through very strong evidence in the previous chapter and will see here, the exact opposite is true. Faithful Christianity continues to plug along and grow. It is doing so globally and will continue to do so well through this century. That is *very* good news.

Our assumption in the Western world is that Islam is on the rise and well on its way to world domination. This is not the case. The assumption exists merely because, as Jenkins explains, "Islam has registered in the last twenty or thirty years only because we see it as politically threatening." He adds, completely tongue-in-cheek, "Maybe some Christians somewhere would have to take hostages before anyone would really notice they're there."[6] The West has been paying great attention to the political influence of Islam due to its dominance in the news, its global politics, the terrorism of its more radical fringes, and its overall immigration movements.

But according to Jenkins, if we look at sheer numbers, quiet Christians own the present, and he asserts Christianity will enjoy a sustained "worldwide boom" throughout our present century. He is speaking of *explosion*, not *implosion*. In fact, Jenkins regularly describes what he sees happening as a *new Christendom*, a term he has coined, because the Christian faith is changing so powerfully around the world, resulting in Christians "leading an epochal cultural revolution."[7]

This brings us to our next two truths Professor Jenkins says must be recognized.

2. Christianity's greatest growth *is* taking place and will *continue* in the Global South.

The *Global South* is a curious term for most people, but sociologists use it commonly to describe an important and unique section of the world. It does not necessarily refer to the world of the southern hemisphere, but rather what many refer to as the "developing world" or the "third world." Primarily these areas of the world are indeed south of the equator, while some lie north of it. Most of us will tend to see, particularly with our Western eyes, mostly bad news coming from these parts of the world. But lots of good things are happening there as well.

The dramatic and explosive growth of Christianity in the Global South is one of the greatest benefits to the people there. Jenkins speaks of this shift in belief as a reformation, every bit as powerful and consequential as the other big one that happened in Germany a few centuries ago. The Protestant Reformation was not just theological or ecclesiological; it had profound cultural consequences in economics, industry, education, the arts, and government. It would be nearly impossible to list all the areas that were impacted by that movement. The same is happening in this reformation of faith in the Global South. In a major cover story Jenkins penned for the *Atlantic*, he wrote that "Christianity as a whole is both growing and mutating in ways that observers in the West tend not to see."[8]

This has been happening slowly but surely for some time. Jenkins asserts in *The Next Christendom* that today, "the center of gravity in the Christian world has shifted inexorably . . . southward, to Africa and Latin America, and eastward, toward Asia." By 2025, half of all Christians in the world will live in Africa and Latin America. He quotes Professor John Mbiti, a Kenyan scholar in religion, who observes that the new "centers of the church's universality [are] no longer in Geneva, Rome, Athens, Paris London, New York, but Kinshasa, Buenos Aires, Addis Ababa and Manila." Jenkins agrees, adding, "Whatever Europeans or North Americans may believe, Christianity is doing very well indeed in the global South—not just surviving but expanding."[9] He often uses the word *booming*, a powerful and hard-to-misunderstand descriptor. Academics are certainly not inclined to use such effusive superlatives, so when they do, it's worth noting.

By 2050, the United States will have more Christians living on its soil than any other country, but a great majority of the other half will be found in the developing world, and the biggest growth dynamic will be there as well. Jenkins lists Mexico, Brazil, Nigeria, the Democratic Republic of the Congo, Ethiopia, and the Philippines as just a few of the places where this will be happening. By 2025, it is likely that almost three-fourths of all Catholic believers on the planet, by far the largest group of Christians globally,[10] will live in Africa, Asia, and Latin America. Jenkins colorfully explains that settling on exact numbers of Christians in the Global South is difficult because the churches there "are too busy baptizing newcomers to be counting them very precisely."[11]

In terms of specific percentages of growth taking place in many of these regions of the world, demographers at Gordon-Conwell Seminary's Center for the Study of Global Christianity have gathered very good numbers. Each of these figures below, which account for increases in total number of Christians, covers the span of time between 1970 to 2017:

- The five regions they track in Africa: 408 percent increase
- The five regions they track in Asia: 324 percent increase
- The three regions they track in Latin America: 124 percent increase
- The four regions they track in Oceania: 71 percent increase

By comparison, the increase in total number of Christians in the United States over this same time: 37 percent.[12] No one can claim that describing what's happening in these global regions as "booming" is an overstatement.

Jenkins gives a lively description of how the church is thriving on our tiny planet:

It would not be very easy to convince a congregation in Seoul or Nairobi that Christianity . . . is dying, when their main concern is building a worship facility big enough for the ten or twenty thousand members they have gained over the past few years. And these new converts are mostly teenagers and young adults, by no means the graying reactionaries of media legend.

Regarding the false and tired "churches must join the modern age in theology and morals or die" mantra from the secularists and theological liberals, Jenkins notes, "Nor can these churches be easily told that, in order to reach a mass audience, they must bring their message more into accord with (Western) secular orthodoxies."[13]

Quite the opposite is happening, which brings us to Jenkins's third point.

3. Christianity's global growth is uncontestably and robustly theologically conservative, traditional, and spiritually dynamic.

If there is one thing that marks this extraordinary growth in the Global South, it's that these movements are strongly conservative in their theology, ecclesiology, and sexual teachings. In many important ways, these believers are much more traditional than those who identify as theological conservatives here in the United States. Jenkins puts it succinctly: "On present evidence, a Southernized Christian future should be distinctly conservative."[14]

Some of this conservative theology is being imported, and will continue to be, to the States. One example is found in two very different forces today within the Anglican tradition. Perhaps you have noted it yourself; maybe you've even been a part of it. If you look around, there are many young evangelicals eager to tell you they're becoming Anglican, and they aren't referring to the Anglicanism of the Global North. What we typically know as Episcopalianism is collapsing with great force. It seems as if this branch of Anglicanism couldn't achieve this fall more efficiently if they sent their parishioners personal invitations to leave *now!* Of course, that invitation is effectively being sent with every vote the denomination's authorities take to jettison various forms of clear biblical teaching.

What so many young evangelicals here and in Europe are joining is the booming Anglicanism being led by the bishops of Africa. These men, who are unflinching stalwarts for the truth, are parting with the larger, northern Anglican Communion over their liberalizing theology and sexuality, primarily the issue of homosexuality. In 2016, a commentator wrote in the British paper, the *Guardian*, that these African bishops who left the Church of England were not so much "leaving the Anglican communion, but walking out of its funeral."[15] They have done more than merely leave. These bold and unapologetic bishops have started nothing short of a revolution. There are now more of these new Anglican churches in Africa than there are Anglican churches in the United Kingdom! They have more seminaries as well. The weight of Anglicanism is shifting in a very clear and decisive direction. Its center is no longer London but Nigeria.

New Anglican churches are springing up in America for the express purpose of aligning themselves with the African bishops' leadership and covering. I cannot count all the friends I have who've joined these churches. As my children have entered young adulthood and are making their own choices about where to attend church, some of them have gone to these Anglican churches. Young adults are seeking and thus moving toward biblical faithfulness and tradition.

John Stonestreet, president of the Colson Center for Christian Worldview, moved with his family from the general evangelicalism of his childhood to the Anglican church that is aligned with these

African bishops. He explains, from his vast observations and experience, that it seems "as if the draw for younger generations to a more structured and ancient expression of Christian worship has to do, at least in part, with a growing desire to connect with something beyond a church brand or strong personality." They are not looking for theological innovations from the church and its leaders or wholly new doctrines for a new age, but for fidelity to a tradition rooted in the authority and life-giving truth of Scripture. Stonestreet adds that "the idea of finding something historic, stable and, in particular, not marketed at them seems to be attractive to many in the younger generation."[16] Again, few are searching for skim-milk Christianity. Not even the young adults today. They are seeking and moving toward the real, robust deal.

Remarkably, the conservatively traditional Nigerian branch of the Anglican church is well on its way to becoming that tradition's most dominant body. Who would have imagined this fifty years ago?

The commitment to conservative theology among these churches in Africa, Asia, Latin America, and Oceania is precisely what brought Jenkins to write his second book on the topic, *The New Faces of Christianity*, giving it the subtitle *Believing the Bible in the Global South*. He opens his first chapter with a telling story of two Anglican priests some years ago attending Bible study together. As they were considering a particular passage, they reached a passionate disagreement on what it meant. The America priest arrogantly told his African colleague that he would do well to see such things from the new naturalistic point of view provided by modern scholarship. However, it was not that the African didn't know about these new "enlightened" methods; it's that he did and rejected them. Finally, in irritation, the African priest asked his Western peer, "If you don't believe the Bible, why did you bring it to us in the first place?"

It's a good question. This is why Archbishop Benjamin Nzimbi of Kenya draws such a stark distinction between these two approaches: "Our understanding of the Bible is different from them. We are two different churches."[17] Their views on the Scriptures are what divide them. Jenkins spells it out forthrightly: "For the foreseeable future . . . the fastest-growing segments of Christianity worldwide will share certain approaches to biblical authority and interpretation."[18]

That approach is decidedly traditional and penetrates all aspects of the church and the Christian life for the majority of believers in Asia, Africa, and Latin America, just as we have seen in the Western world. They take the Scriptures at face value and believe what they say. People in these nations are flocking to these pastors' fidelity to God's Word and their impassioned practical teaching on how it can change lives. They do not want a gospel totally gutted by the spineless and reconstituted liberalism that cannot meet their needs.

Liberalizing movements brought dramatic efforts of arrogant and paternalistic theological Western colonialism upon these bishops. It is not too hard to imagine that these clergy are seen as backward and uneducated by their Western-educated peers because of their supposedly throwback views of the Bible. Pay no attention to the fact that many of these African bishops were educated in leading Western institutions. And ironically, for progressives who contend they are deeply sensitive about exporting imperialist Western ways to the third world, they don't seem shy about demanding submission to their radically new sexual ethics from these believers. Here are just two stark and absolutely stunning examples.

At a meeting of liberal clergy in San Francisco some years ago, one conferee pointed out that "those African bishops" were the primary problem in the church today and they needed to be "dealt with." Goodness. At another gathering in New York City on the topic of ordaining gay clergy in the Anglican church, a deeply frustrated white, gay Episcopalian announced in his session that the African bishops must stop "monkeying around" with the rest of the church and said these very words: "All I have to say to these bishops is: Go back to the jungle where you came from."[19] Okay then. Rank bigotry in the name of "progress." So much for enlightened tolerance and inclusion.

These growing churches in the Global South are not just theologically conservative but are also remarkably dynamic in terms of their spiritual practice and experiences. First, Jenkins explains, these "newer churches preach deep personal faith and communal orthodoxy, mysticism and puritanism, all founded on clear scriptural authority." Many of their practices could seem simplistic and terribly antiquated to a patriarchal and elitist Western mind-set, but they clearly appeal to the masses. Jenkins observes that "prophecy is an everyday reality, while faith-healing, exorcism, and dream-visions are all fundamental parts" of their practice and experience.[20] These believers also hold a very real and sincere belief of Jesus as truly God, acting personally and intimately in the lives of people, overcoming sin and all manner of evil forces. Anyone the least bit familiar with Jesus's experiences in the Gospels and the early church in the book of Acts will easily recognize these things as everyday life at that time. That's true for these churches today as well. There's no way to see that as a bad thing.

From his vast work, Jenkins confidently concludes that "there can be no doubt about the underlying realities, demographic and religious, which ensure that Christianity will flourish in the near future." The results of this growing Christianity are believers who maintain careful biblical fidelity, spiritual vibrancy, and a deeply supernatural orientation, and great evangelistic success in lives being forever changed in radical ways.[21]

Professor Jenkins is certainly not alone in this take on global Christianity. Many others have noted the growth and vibrancy of faith in the Global South as well.

Professor Rodney Stark, a colleague of Jenkins's at Baylor University, has found the same thing in his research. He reports that Christians in the southern regions of the African continent are deeply Christianized and practice their faith with much more energy and zeal than they did their old tribal religions. Church attendance across these regions is as high, if not higher, than anywhere else in the world. Consider the growth among Catholics in Africa. In 1960, just over two thousand men were preparing for the priesthood in seminary. By 2011, the number had swollen to well over twenty-seven thousand seminarians. That's explosive growth.

Specifically, 90 percent of Nigerians report having attended Protestant or Catholic services, and not just attended at some time during the year. Ninety percent attended in the past week that the survey was taken! These are not sleepy, cultural Christians. Botswana has the region's lowest church attendance . . . with 49 percent of its citizens having attended church in the last week! On average, 71 percent of the people in sub-Saharan Africa attend church weekly. Stark explains these services are generally not sedate, somber affairs, even among the Anglicans, but "resemble what most Westerners would call a revival meeting." God is worshiped with great fervency, people are saved, illnesses are healed, and demons are sent packing. It's muscular Christianity. "In short," Stark adds, "southern Africa has undergone a seismic religious shift" both in terms of numbers and spiritual passion.[22]

John Micklethwait and Adrian Wooldridge, both Oxford educated senior journalists for the *Economist*, wrote a well-researched book some years back entitled *God Is Back: How the Global Revival of Faith Is Changing the World*. Even though they use the word *faith*, their book is about Christianity. They did not come up with the title of their book casually.

In its last edition of the second millennium, the *Economist* ceremoniously published God's obituary. Of course, God's death is big news by any measure, so the editors were sure to let their readers know that "after a lengthy career, the Almighty recently passed into history."[23] However, the *Economist* was surprised to find in 2007 that He had apparently risen from the dead, as God had done once before. That was when they published a cover story entitled "In God's Name: A Special Report on Religion and Public Life." It was a miracle!

In 2009, Micklethwait and Wooldridge determined this good news was so important, it deserved more than just an article; it warranted an entire book. Thus, their bold and declarative title, which they admit was a swipe at the original obit of December 1999. The two journalists spent a great deal of time focusing on China and how Christianity is spreading across that country like a tsunami. But instead of destruction, Christianity is bringing life and drawing in people across all socioeconomic classes, even the well-educated and materially prosperous. In fact, Micklethwait and Woolridge assert that "the growth of Christianity is . . . the most startling religious development" in growing world powers like China. [24]

Economic openness in China is boosting a demand for religion, and both Protestant and Catholic Christianity are filling the void. The Chinese government's own figures show the number of Christians rising from 14 million in 1997 to 21 million in 2006. The authors correctly imagine the real numbers being much higher, offering a "conservative guess" of at least 65 million Protestants and 12 million Catholics currently in China. This means there are more Chinese citizens pledging themselves to Christianity than to the Communist Party. That is what we call a cultural revolution.

Some local Chinese Christians estimate believers to number well over 100 million. Professor Fenggang Yang, a sociologist who founded and heads up the Center on Religion and Chinese Society at Purdue University, estimates the number of Chinese Protestant Christians alone range from 93 to 115 million. The United States' Council on Foreign Relations reports that the population of Protestants in China has grown by an average of 10 percent each year since 1979, thus referring to China's four decade-long growth in Christianity as a "religious revival."[25]

Many of the student leaders who organized and initiated the brave and historic 1989 Tiananmen Square protests have become

Christians, and strong ones at that. One of these young leaders, Zhang Boli, became one of the Chinese government's most wanted criminals against the State due to his leadership at Tiananmen. He escaped China right after the massacre and now pastors a church in the United States. He recalled recently that "China has never experienced such fast progress of Christianity."[26] He said this is due to the collapse of any other larger, life-filling value system that the Chinese people can live by. They are not following the communist philosophy because they have found it wholly inadequate, if not repressive.

People are giving themselves to Christ and His church in such waves that the Chinese government began to get very aggressive against the faith in 2014. Pastor Boli explains how the government started taking down crosses on top of churches and removing crucifixes from inside, as if real Christianity exists in these symbols. Many churches have simply been demolished, razed to the ground and the debris scooped up and hauled off to the garbage dumps, not leaving a trace.

Leaders of house churches are put under house arrest or sentenced to jail. The government started doing background checks on all government employees to make sure none of them are involved in Christian activities. They have also blocked their citizens from buying Christian books and other products online. Christianity has been getting "out of control" there, and the government is taking that fact terribly seriously. But of course these actions have not killed the church, as it is not in the buildings but in the people. Pastor Boli says that many of these churches just renamed themselves and popped up elsewhere.

We must note the obvious here: a government doesn't attempt to eradicate that which is in decline. They go after things that are growing at such remarkable rates that they feel threatened by them. This is the case with Christianity—both Protestant and Catholic—in China, and this growth shows no sign of slowing whatsoever. Despite the aggressive crackdown by the government, Boli is not downcast:

I'm still optimistic about the development of Christianity in China. I'm optimistic because of what I saw being the growth of Christianity from 1989 till now. This is the wonderful work that God has done. And also, the wonderful leading of the Holy Spirit in China because the Chinese churches are not largely supported by Western churches, they grow mostly by themselves.[27]

For all the talk about how the twentieth century was to find Christianity in the grave, as the *Economist* declared at the end of 1999, their own journalists appreciate the great contrast between expectation and reality.

Today an unsettling worry nags at Western liberals: what if secular Europe (and for that matter secular Harvard and secular Manhattan) is the odd one out? They are right to be worried. It now seems that it is the American model [of Christianity] that is spreading around the world: religion and modernity are going hand in hand, not just in China but throughout much of Asia, Africa, Arabia and Latin America.[28]

Micklethwait and Woolridge are speaking of the "American model" as more faithfully vibrant and scripturally orthodox, distinct from the gutless, secularized European experience. They continue, pointing out the surprising irony of a totally unexpected synergy between some important consequences of modernity and the practice of the ancient faith: "It is not just that religion is thriving in many modernizing countries; it is also that [Christianity] is succeeding in harnessing the tools of modernity to propagate its message. The very things that were supposed to destroy religion—democracy and markets, technology and reason—are combining to make it stronger."[29]

God Is Back explains how more countries are following the American model of Christianity and freedom than the European model of secularism and state control: "The American model of religion—one that is based on choice rather than state fiat—is winning."[30]

Christianity around the world is doing more than okay. It would be the rare company or institution that would not wish for the kind of growth Christianity is seeing across the globe in terms of both numbers, innovation of outreach and passion of its adherents.

WHY THE TREMENDOUS GROWTH IN THE GLOBAL SOUTH?

As we have seen, there are many factors driving this expansive growth. Of course, we as Christians understand that it is the Holy Spirit who takes the truth of God where He wills and lays it upon the heart of men, women, and children. The Holy Spirit will never be thwarted in this, as we will discuss in the final chapter of this book. But we can also look at some sociological factors that contribute to the worldwide growth of the church that are important to understand as well, which are also part of the Holy Spirit's work.

First, as the authors of *God Is Back* recognize, Christianity adapts very well from culture to culture. It does this much more effectively and easily than other major faiths like Islam, Buddhism, Hinduism, and even orthodox Judaism because Christianity blends into and strengthens a particular culture.

Unlike Islam, Christianity does not demand a dramatic change in terms of dress and geographical allegiance. The dramatic changes in faith and life practice that Christianity requires can, and should, be integrated easily in every people group's own culture. Asian converts remain Asian. Irish converts remain Irish. Guatemalan converts remain Guatemalan. Southern Californian converts remain Southern Californians. In a very significant way, this makes Christianity *the* largest, most diverse and inclusive group of people on the face of the planet.

Another factor to look at is conversion rates. As we have seen, more traditional, conservative biblical Christianity takes seriously Christ's command to share His good news with all peoples. Thus, these believers are very committed, strategic, and creative in doing this. Today, less than 4 percent of all missionaries are sent by the more liberal, mainstream churches. *Less than 4 percent.* People who don't really believe in what they are supposed to believe don't tend to be excited about sharing that (un)belief with others. "Thus," as Rodney Stark explains, "Protestantism in Africa is overwhelmingly conservative." Faithfully biblical churches are the ones sending out their members to grow the church, causing conservative churches to split at the seams and new churches to crop up with regularity. This is a trend we are seeing across the world. The march of the church will not be staunched, and when outside forces try to stop it, it only grows even more.

The third area to consider is one that very few people think about, but sociologists know it's a major player in the growth of faith: *fertility*. It comes down to who's having the babies. In a major report on the changing landscape of religion throughout the world, the Pew Research Center noted in 2017 that fertility among a particular faith's adherents was a major driver of that faith's growth. It is a sociological truism that for the most part, the way kids are raised—the practices and beliefs strongly held and lived out in their childhood home—greatly impacts what they will tend to be and believe as adults. If one grows up in a Christian, Muslim, Buddhist, vegan, cowboy, sailing, surfing, hunting, reading, or gardening home, it is very likely he or she will continue with that belief, practice, or tradition in their own home to varying degrees. It's what humans tend to do. And the more children who grow up in that home, the more people who will go out into the world doing those things. So one very fertile generation of faithful Christians will make a very strong and important contribution to the existence of the next generation of faithful Christians just by making babies and parenting them well.

In the very first sentence of the 2017 report *The Changing Global Religious Landscape*, Pew proclaims, "More babies were born to Christian mothers than to members of any other religion in recent years, reflecting Christianity's continued status as the world's largest religious group." However, they state in the next sentence that Muslim fertility is expected to move slightly ahead of Christians in fewer than twenty years from now. Pew predicts that because of this, Muslims will replace Christianity as the fastest *growing* faith in the world in the coming decades. But Christianity will still be the world's *largest* faith and Professor Jenkins holds that this will continue throughout most of this century.

Another important factor in religious growth and decline is what's happening on the other end of life span: death rates. Christianity has a higher projected death rate than Muslims because its population is generally older. But Christianity's robust fertility rate will counter this. Pew tells us that the number of Christians in the world will continue to grow by 34 percent between now and 2060, staying ahead of population growth. They project that in 2060, in disagreement with Jenkins, the worldwide Muslim population will catch up with the Christian population via fertility.[31] No other religious faith, especially the nones or atheists, will come close to keeping up with population growth, much less keep up with Christianity or Islam. The future belongs to either one of these faiths. It certainly does not belong to those with no faith.

The nones who are supposed to be dominating the faith scene in the coming decades are having very few babies. By 2055 or so, only 9 percent of all births will be to parents with no religious affiliation, while 36 percent of babies will be born to Muslims and 35 percent will be born to Christian parents. The nones will be declining significantly in the coming decades, even though 62 percent of Americans wrongly predict the nones will be growing. Only 15 percent think they will decrease. This is because the majority has been listening uncritically to the news that the future belongs to the secularists and the past belongs to Christians. You can fool most of the people some of the time, but there's no reason they have to remain fooled.

The University of London's Eric Kaufmann agrees with Pew and Jenkins. He explains in his important book *Shall the Religious Inherit the Earth?* (he says they will indeed) that the sustaining vitality and even significant per capita growth of serious Christian belief is as firmly rooted in fertility as it is in faithful teaching and evangelism. This is something the church cannot miss. He puts it bluntly: "The secular West and East Asia are aging and their share of the world population declining." The Christians are not. He continues, "This means the world is getting more religious even as people in the rich world shed their faith."[32]

Social scientists and demographers have predicted Christianity will still be strong throughout this century. But so will Islam. However, projections are not reality. Thus, as Orthodox theologian David Bentley Hart correctly proclaimed in *First Things*, the most "subversive and effective strategy we [Christians] might undertake [to counter the culture] would be one of militant fecundity: abundant, relentless, exuberant, and defiant childbearing."[33]

The future belongs to the fertile, and Christians must realize that an important way to fulfill the Great Commission happens in the bedroom and the birthing room. Christians can easily change these projections in some very important and absolutely delightful ways so that Christianity stays the dominant faith well beyond the twenty-first century. We can do this by turning our own parents into grandparents, and doing so about three times or more. That's not so hard, and your parents will be beside themselves.

Bottom line: Christianity, and the right kind of Christianity, is exploding around the world and will continue to do so for the foreseeable future. Anyone who knows C. S. Lewis's *Chronicles of Narnia* series even remotely can agree heartily with Mr. Beaver that "Aslan is on the move." Indeed He is, and the best research gives that fact every support.

CHAPTER 7

ARE YOUNG PEOPLE REALLY LEAVING THE CHURCH?

In early 2019, I googled two precise phrases related to the idea that teens and young adults are leaving Christianity and the church in disturbing numbers. The phrase "young people leaving Christianity" garnered 463 results according to Google's analytics. The even more precise but obviously more often used phrase "young people are leaving the church in droves" produced 6,980 results. These phrases showed up in about 7,500 articles, news stories, blog posts, and other media! There is clearly a great deal of talk about this subject and a great deal of fear that it's true. But is it?

It is essential that we address this topic in relation to our young people specifically for two important reasons: (1) they are our children, and (2) they are the future of the church.

Some might admit that sure, Christianity and the church are growing nicely around the world, but young people are indeed leaving the church. We believe it because so many smart and authoritative people say it's true. But it is not true, quite the contrary. The news regarding our young adults is very good and should be very encouraging for parents who are serious about their faith and churches that teach and practice a vibrant and biblically faithful Christianity. The sky is not falling, but is actually quite secure.

Before we dive in, we must note that teens and young adults have *always* tended to be less faithful in their religious participation than their parents, or at least less faithful than their parents wish them to be. In Jesus's day, in the early church, during the Reformation, for the Puritans, for your great grandparents, right up today. Emerging and young adults act like they have a mind of their own, but those kids always become adults who doubt the real dedication of the next generation. "Kids these days!" is not a new complaint. It's the course of nature.

But it seems of late that many evangelicals have become quite freaked out over this common cycle. As we saw in the introduction of this book, there are widely proclaimed and believed claims that there might not even be a church in ten or twenty years because young people are checking out by the gazillions. These warnings have been made for years, and here we are still.

Baylor's Rodney Stark has long pointed out that the five-alarm warning of declining faith practice among our youth is a wholesale false alarm. As we saw at the beginning of chapter 2, he also is not shy about expressing his frustration that this false claim continues to be repeated as fact, explaining that many of those claiming the church is sinking are making a living off of the news "and they're always wrong."[1] It's not true.

In his book *What Americans Really Believe*, Stark explains that "this same effect can be found in *every* national survey of church attendance ever done. Young people have always been less likely to attend church than are older people." And Stark adds, "That [young adults] haven't defected from the church is obvious from the fact that a bit later in life, when they have married, especially after children arrive, they become more regular attenders. This happens every generation."[2]

For fun, he adds, "That's been going on I suppose since Cain and Abel." Yes, murdering your brother might qualify as "walking away from the faith." This cooling of church attendance often happens when our kids go off to college. They've gained their independence and are ready to experience all the life opportunities that go along with that freedom. They have new school schedules and pressures. College life is more demanding. Their social and work lives have changed, typically meaning they have later, longer Saturday evenings, which translates into groggy Sunday mornings of lying prostrate in the Church of the Downy Comforter or faithfully attending Bedtime Baptist.

But what about actual church attendance of young adults over the last few decades in real numbers? Have we seen a decline here, a precipitous, apocalyptic one?

First of all, we must know that every generation, among all age groups, in all socioeconomic categories, sees dips and rises in all measures of faith practice. This is true of anything in human behavior that can be measured. There are annual dips and declines in the number of people who eat carrots or go to the grocery for milk and bread every other day. Everything dips, declines, and rises at varying levels, even death and taxes. So it's the decades-long trends that tell the fuller story regarding church attendance and faith affiliation for all age groups. That is what we will look at here.

Wheaton College's Ed Stetzer is among the small group of scholars around the world doing strong and consistent academic work specifically in the area of young adults. While interviewing Stetzer, he explained to me some very important data from the University of Chicago's universally respected General Social Survey (GSS). He said, "If you look at young [evangelical] adults, eighteen to twenty-nine years old, we are at the highest reported levels since 1972 of *regular* church attendance among this group. That's a pretty big deal." It is indeed. He added, "What all this means is there is certainly *not* an evangelical collapse," not even among young people. Additionally, the percentage of young adults in this age group who self-identify as evangelicals doubled from 1972 to 2016, the last year for which the GSS has data.

This is not polling done by some Christian groups here and there who don't really do academic, broad population research. These results come from the very data that all professional sociologists rely on for their own diverse and complex research in demographics in the United States. And this survey's findings are clear: more young people are attending evangelical churches today than they have in quite a long time; more than twice as many who did forty years ago. That qualifies nicely as the exact opposite of "leaving in droves."

Professor Bradley Wright, a sociologist from the University of Connecticut, explains that nationally representative data from annual surveys of high school seniors—the widely respected Monitoring the Future project from the University of Michigan—reveals that since the early 1980s, this group has remained largely stable in their answers to questions like "How important is religion in your life?" and "How often do you attend church?" The percentage of high school seniors who answer "pretty important" or "somewhat important" on the place of faith in their lives and "pretty often" or "somewhat often" on the attendance question have all held steady for the last few decades.[3]

Byron Johnson, distinguished professor of the social sciences and co-director with Rodney Stark of the Institute for Studies of Religion at Baylor University, has carefully followed faith trends among young people for decades. Like Professors Wright, Stetzer, and Stark, he is more positive about the current picture of things, explaining,

The number of evangelicals remains high, and their percentage among practicing Christians in America is, if anything, rising. Young evangelicals are not turning to more liberal positions on controversial social issues; in some cases they are becoming more conservative than their parents. . . . Those who argue that a new American landscape is emerging—one in which conservative evangelicalism of the past few decades is losing numbers and influence—are simply ignoring the data.[4]

Christian Smith, the director of the Center for the Study of Religion and Society and the director of the Notre Dame Center for Social Research, is the uncontested leader in this field of study of young adults and faith. He agrees with these conclusions of the general stability of young adults' faith through the last few decades. He finds that "emerging adults today appear no less religious than those of previous decades . . . when it comes to daily prayer, Bible beliefs and strong religious affiliation," adding, "Not much appears to have changed." Thus, "on the whole" he says, "18- to 24-year-old Americans have not since 1972 become dramatically less religious or more secular."[5] Smith adds some additional and surprising good news here:

> Most emerging adults *themselves* report little change in how religious they have been in the in the previous five years. And those who do report change are more likely to say they have become *more*, not less, religious.[6]

Two other respected scholars in this field show largely the same thing. Lisa D. Pearce and Melinda Denton report in their book, *A Faith of Their Own*, that faith among adolescents has remained stable over the last few decades. In agreement with Smith, they found that youth who did experience some change were inclined to report being stronger in their faith.

This good news is further strengthened when these researchers tell us that "between 70 and 80 percent of adolescents who attend religious services find their religious congregations to be warm and welcoming and report that they usually inspire them to think." Pearce and Denton elaborate with a finding that is very much at odds with the current narrative, "Far less common are youth who are affiliated with but not engaged by congregations."[7] Thus, they are saying that the "nones" are rare creatures among teens and young adults. The data shows us that the picture of young people is very positive in faithful evangelical families and churches. This contradicts the belief, held by many, that if young people do stick to their Christian faith, they are not as likely to attend church, finding it largely irrelevant. This is just not the case.

In addition, the people at the Pew Research Center report that millennials are a bit more likely to pray every day than their peers growing up in the 1980s and '90s.[8]

Percentage of Young Adults Who Pray Daily
(by decade)

	1980s	1990s	2000s
pray daily	41	40	45
pray less often	59	60	55

Pew elaborates that among millennials *"who are affiliated with a religion . . .* the intensity of their religious affiliation is as strong today as among previous generations when they were young." The number of millennials who report being a "strong" member of their faith community are in line with number of Gen Xers but actually slightly higher than Boomers were at the same age.[9] And let us reiterate, this is what Stetzer saw in the General Social Survey data. The percentage of evangelical eighteen- to twenty-nine-year-olds *doubled* between 1972 and 2016.

Our young people are moving in a particular direction in notable numbers, and it's certainly not away from the doors of evangelical churches. Like Professor Stark, we should start getting irritated with and correct people when we hear false stats being presented as fact. Despite being a people of truth, we certainly can believe and pass around falsehoods as well as anyone. I'll say it again, we should be known for being born again, not born yesterday.

Let's end this examination of young people with perhaps the most important fact regarding the longevity of their faith. It has to do with what kind of home they come from and the kind of faith practiced there. In their *Faith in Flux* report, Pew states that of all who left Christianity as adults, only 12 percent of Catholics and Protestants reported having any kind of strong or serious faith when they were teens.[10] Nearly 90 percent of kids who came from a serious (but not perfect) Christian home, took their faith seriously, and lived it out as best they could carried that faith into adulthood. Kids do tend to hang onto the beliefs and practices their parents gave them. These are precisely true when it comes to the Christian faith. Professor Christian Smith finds the same from his decades of research, explaining, "Highly religious teenagers are not very likely to become very unreligious five years later."[11]

This finding is very significant for all parents and church workers. Teens who have a vibrant, growing faith in their youth and teen years are extremely likely, nearly guaranteed, to retain that faith in adulthood. We will see the larger body of detailed research on just how true this is in the following chapter. You will be both surprised and encouraged to see that accomplishing this very important goal is neither rocket science nor a crapshoot. It's a very encouraging story.

CHAPTER 8

PASSING FAITH TO OUR KIDS IS NEITHER A CRAPSHOOT NOR ROCKET SCIENCE

With all the Chicken Little squawking about young people and the church, it is no wonder that Christian parents are a bit freaked out if not absolutely discouraged and maybe despondent. The story that has been presented is really bad so the conclusion can only be that the odds are against you, and all your hard work is likely to be for naught. But as we have seen in every chapter so far, the truth of the matter is dramatic. It's just the opposite kind of dramatic than what we assume.

In this chapter I hope to encourage parents, extended family, family friends, and church staff by giving a number of relatively simple things that nearly ensure our young people will develop a living and lasting faith in their youth and into adulthood. The research making this case has been presented in the academic books written by university scholars, but it has not appeared in a popular book. Until now.

We will start out with an overview of the best available university-based, academically published research rather than resting on one or two individual studies done by Christian ministries, which nearly all of the "sky is falling" books limit themselves to. We will see the convincing case this research makes about the high likelihood that good, genuine faith from parents and grandparents begets good, genuine faith in their children and grandchildren. We will explore the very effective and relatively simple parental practices and attitudes that contribute to a living and lasting faith among our children.

The advice and direction offered here is practicality based, explaining the most important tasks we as parents can do to help our children develop a vibrant and lasting faith into adulthood. The likelihood of succeeding at this is more certain than you imagine and far less complicated or tricky than you might assume. That is certainly news you'll want to share with your friends, family, and church staff who are laboring to pass on their Christian faith to the next generation.

What parent or Christian worker is not interested in that?

The best research is surprisingly and absolutely consistent and unequivocal about what the number one resource in the successful transmission of faith is and why it is as singularly effective as it is. The first factor is:

1. Parents

Let us see how it rates among the next three things that nearly guarantee our children will take a living and lasting faith with them into adulthood. These are:

2. Parents
3. Parents
4. Parents

And these are followed by the next two most important:

5. Parents
6. Parents

So . . . in summation, what factor is more important and influential than any other in this process? Okay, parents, I know you're freaking out right now, thinking, *What? My children's spiritual well-being, development, and eternal destiny rely primarily on me, like, six times over? Thanks for the pressure. Just what I needed! I'm done with this book now, thank you very much.*

Ironically, it is this very concern that makes you the most consequential player here. It's because you care the most. But you can relax, because the key things parents should do are likely things you are already doing or would be happy to do if you knew how significant they were. You just need the encouragement and confidence that what you are doing really does matter and will make a difference.

But first, I want to let you know that there is no complicated spiritual formula that you must get just right. There are no special products you need to buy, no programs or conferences you need to sign up for or attend. Everything you need is already available to you, and anyone can do the things we will discuss below, regardless of your education level, employment, income, social status, neighborhood, or denomination. None of this requires you to be a spiritual superhero. There is a great deal of grace in this process, and, according to this research, it's actually quite likely you will succeed nicely.

Here's the bottom line: *the things that successful parents do in faith transmission are not rocket science, and the payoff for doing them is eternal.* If this doesn't come under the category of good news for any Christian parent, I'm not sure what does. (And as we shall see, for those of you who are not parents but who come alongside your friends' kids, those at your church, or your nieces and nephews with spiritual direction and influence: you also have a tremendously important second-line-of-defense role in building lasting faith, so don't lose interest, thinking it's all just about parents.)

So let's break down the rest of this chapter into two key sections:

1. How do we know parents matter so substantially?
2. What do successful parents actually do to be successful?

WHY PARENTS?

Parents, whether you realize it or not, you are the most powerful force in molding, challenging, encouraging, and directing your children. It certainly may not seem like it, but you are. I know, you think your kids never listen to what you have to say, and you often feel totally at odds with them. Most parents feel this way. I know that I certainly do with my five young adult kids from time to time. But you are influencing them, and most likely for the good.

But we are all far more critical and needed than we believe. I don't know of one survey asking teens who the most important, impactful people in their lives are where "parents" is not listed as the number one answer. They don't list their friends that highly. Even an MTV poll from a number of years ago found this! Young people consistently say their parents are more important to their development, character, and sense of the world than their closest friends, musicians, actors, teachers, sports stars, anyone! In fact, one respected specialist commented, "Most adolescents still very badly want the loving input and engagement of their parents—more, in fact, than most parents ever realize." So, if our kids don't actually know *everything*, it appears they do know *some* things that we ourselves have a hard time grasping. Parents matter, and no other person can replace you. So chin up.

Let's dive into the research.

Two of the largest and most long-term studies ever conducted on young people and faith development—one from the University of Southern California and the other from the University of North Carolina at Chapel Hill—both emphasize without fear of overstatement how critical they found parent involvement to be.

Dr. Vern Bengtson, working from USC, presents the collective findings of his four-decade-long investigation into this matter in his book *Families and Faith: How Religion Is Passed Down Across Generations*. A celebrated sociologist said Bengtson's book "fills me with awe" in its "magnitude." That is high praise.

Professor Bengtson confidently states in the book's conclusion that in terms of passing on their faith to their children and follow-ing generations, "Religious families are surprisingly successful at transmission."[1] What's more, he finds the strong influence parents have in passing this baton of faith to their children has not declined since the 1970s, despite the tremendous and tumultuous changes we have seen in our culture's values! Things continue to get bad in our culture, but parents' influence remains strong. He explains,

One result of such cultural, familial and religious [liberaliz-ing] trends has been, according to many religious and social commentators, an erosion of the moral and religious influ-ence of families [i.e., parents]. With our longitudinal data on religion on both parents and young adult children, we could examine if this was true. *To our surprise, it was not.*[2]

Professor Bengtson continues,

In short, our results indicate that the decline of parental influ-ence assumed by many has not occurred in religious belief and practices. Rather than rebelling against or abandon-ing their parents' values and beliefs, a majority of younger-generation members today appear to have retained those values and beliefs—while also adapting them into a new historical context.

This last statement is extremely important. Can you see why? Not only have our kids tended to adopt our faith; they have also adapted it to their own generational situation. I have seen this in my own kids. This ability to adapt their parents and grandparents' faith to their own generational context implies a stronger and more sophisticated grasp of that faith than we might assume. They are not just buying their parents' faith "off the rack," if you will, but taking the essential substance of it and living it out in the unique situation of their own generation. That was true of past generations, and it is still true today. It's like knowing a song so well that you can take it and improvise it in a way that connects with a very different audience and age. That reflects a strong and confident command of the song itself. It is often the same with our children's grasp of their own faith.

If you grew up with a serious Christian faith, when you think back in your late teens and early twenties, it is likely you remember you lived it out a bit differently than your parents. But parents are indeed the prime movers, even if you don't always feel that is true. Of course, the Holy Spirit Himself is the real agent here but you are His primary earthly tool.

Professor Christian Smith, working from his own massive multi-year, several-million-dollar study—the National Study of Youth and Religion (NSYR)—explained in a lecture, given a few years ago at Focus on the Family, that "parents are huge—*absolutely huge*—nearly a necessary condition" for a child to adopt a living and lasting faith. He concludes, "Without question, the most important pastor a child will ever have in their life is a parent." As we have noted before through these pages, academic sociologists are not often given to such absolute statements, so it's worth noting when they make them.

And what is very encouraging is the quality and vibrancy of that faith he finds parents passing on. His findings showed that fully 85 percent of teens raised by parents who took their faith very seriously, and lived in a home with consistent faith practices, became young adults who not only had a serious faith, but had the *highest* levels of religious belief and practice among their peers! This is a remarkable finding, so read it again slowly and take it in. Eight-five percent of teens raised by faithful parents will not just hang on to their faith but are likely to be *very* strong Christians. We have certainly not heard that among all the bad news. But it comes from an impeccable source.

Professor Smith makes another dramatic statement regarding his team's findings. He says the connection between parents' influence on their children's faith development "is nearly deterministic."[3] Nearly deterministic. Again, note the strong, absolute language he uses here. He's not using it for affect. Scholars don't do that. He's using it because it accurately describes what he found. Smith concludes, "Highly religious teenagers are not very likely to become very unreligious five years later" in their early adult years.[4]

There are numerous studies beyond these two 150-pound gorillas showing the same things on the unchallenged importance parents play in faith transmission. We won't review all of them here, but two such studies stand out and are worth noting. Research from Penn State University reports "that adult [child] *religiosity is determined largely by parental religiosity*" and "that parental influences have considerable staying power even as offspring move out of the home and form independent households."[5]

Another scholarly essay on the transmission of religious belief across generations published in a book by Johns Hopkins University Press affirms that across ethnic groups, "the quality of intergenerational relations and the closeness of parent-child relationships is perhaps the strongest predictor of religious continuity across generations."[6]

What can we then conclude? *Like begets like.*

Parents with a weak faith or no faith at all tend to produce children with weak or no faith. Parents who hold and practice a vibrantly strong and attractive faith tend to produce children who have a vibrant and attractive faith. Parents can do this like no one else.

How different is this news from what you've heard in church circles over the past few years? It surprised even the scholars themselves. So all this is good news for our young people and good news for you as faithful parents. Your role in your children's lives is profound, and what you have been doing is not for nothing, even it seems the exact opposite is true. Take both confidence and encouragement in that. It would take a whole army of additional spiritual resources to replace your influence in this essential work, if they could replace you at all. You're the Billy Graham in your kids' lives, even if you don't have his booming voice and unique accent. And your impact comes most powerfully and effectively from you having a close, warm relationship with your kids and living out your Christianity faithfully, if not always perfectly, week by week, year by year before them. In fact, your imperfection can have a very positive influence itself. No one likes someone who never makes mistakes. But we do like people who make mistakes, face them honestly, and use them to better themselves. We gain encouragement from and learn to admire such people. Your children will do the same with you.

We know the falsehood and danger in parents who practice "do as I say, not as I do." The consistency between what we believe as parents and what we do is critical in terms of the important spiritual notes our kids unconsciously take from us. To use the well-worn but true phrase, *it is more important to walk the walk than talk the talk.*

But there's data that offers a curious challenge to this. Of course our children are more likely to adopt our faith when there is a consistency between what our mouths and feet do, when they see our pronounced faith lived out in real ways. But research done jointly from Baylor and Purdue Universities found that children raised by parents who put a high importance on faith in the home but showed low attendance in faith activities . . .

exhibited significantly higher levels of church attendance, attached more importance to religion, prayed with greater frequency and had more conservative views of the Bible. In other words, parents who believe religion to be very important tend to have more religious kids, even if those parents do not attend church regularly.

In contrast, these scholars explain,

In simple terms, parents who ascribe low importance to religion will be less likely to transmit religious behaviors and values to their children, even if the family attends church regularly.[7]

Is this your research-based excuse for not going to church? Certainly not. These scholars only convey this information to drive home the point of the importance of parents' own dedication to their faith in the home. If you had to choose between attending church or your own spiritual leadership as the most important influence upon your child, it is the latter. But you don't have to choose one or the other. Your child can and should benefit from the strong influence of both.

What I take away as great encouragement from this collective research is that we don't have to be super Christians to succeed at passing on our faith to our children. We can fail from time to time, as we all do, and still succeed. We just have to be consistently clear in meaningful ways, in the midst of our many mistakes and short-comings, how important our faith is to us. Authenticity and genuine-ness are more powerful than the false veneer of perfection. Remember that. Our kids can so easily see the difference. And they do. When I see our kids persevering in their faith, I wonder how it can be, because I know I made so many mistakes and missteps in raising them in their faith. But God is gracious, and our kids have a great ability to divide the mistakes we make from our actual selves. If we get it right a few more times than we get it wrong, our kids are likely to be in good shape. No one is keeping score. It's about how we do in the long game overall.

So what are the things parents should be doing to put them in the circle of greater success?[8] We will examine these now, and you can be encouraged because they don't require a seminary degree. Not even close.

HIGHLY SUCCESSFUL PARENTS CONNECT WITH THEIR KIDS

So, what is it that parents actually do to succeed in passing on their faith? This is a critical question, and there are encouraging and consistent answers. Let's look.

First, parents who are directive, warm, and have not only clearly and effectively communicated expectations for their children but back these expectations up have the greatest success in passing along their faith. In fact, Professor Bengtson finds that this relational closeness, loving directedness, and affirmation practiced by the parent is so important he dedicated an entire chapter to the topic in his book. He entitled it simply "The Importance of Warmth." Christian Smith and his team found this was the single most important overarching aspect as well.

Children who feel close to and secure with their parents who are faithful Christians are at least twice as likely, and by some measures more so, to have a more passionate personal and public faith, higher levels of church and faith-life participation, and more biblically faithful views and convictions than their peers who do not have such parents who are Christians. Bengtson explains that "within tightknit religious traditions such as [Evangelicalism and Judaism], the chances of passing on faith are highly dependent on the quality of parent-child relationships."

Research from the University of Texas at Austin also finds that the health, security, and sense of connectedness that children find in their relationship with their parents translates into a deeper and more vibrant faith in the lives of teens and remains consistent as they move into adulthood. These scholars explain that "higher family satisfaction . . . predicts higher adolescent religiosity."[9] *Predicts* is a strong word they've chosen to use, rare for social scientists who usually use looser language such a "tends to" or "is related to."

TEACHING AND MODELING
SPIRITUAL DISCIPLINES IS VITAL

Not surprisingly, studies repeatedly show that teens who develop a few important spiritual disciplines are very likely to carry those practices into their young adult years and beyond in meaningful ways. They create a spiritual rootedness that sticks with them.

Two of the most critical disciplines are regular prayer and a practice of and appreciation for reading the Scriptures. Our kids must develop a love for these things for themselves and in their own ways. Kids cannot be forced to do them as a rigid "must do" discipline, like practicing the piano for thirty minutes every day. As we know, that approach will actually backfire. We must slowly and carefully help them develop an appreciation and habit within themselves rather than force it upon them from the outside. They must also learn that sometimes they won't *feel* like doing these things, but getting up and doing them anyway is important, just like many of the best things in life.

There are seven primary disciplines or experiences, including prayer and reading God's Word, that faith-steady children develop, and they vary in degrees of importance. Here we go.

1. Prayer

Studies have consistently found that teens who have developed a life of daily and relatively consistent personal prayer—something they gain for themselves, hopefully from earliest ages, as a natural part of their lives—are likely to carry this practice into early adulthood and beyond. What good is a spiritual life if there is not growing intimacy in regular prayer with God, right?

Our kids "catch" this from their parents (and others, as we will see later). In fact—and this is important—they are more likely to catch this from parents who do *not* do it perfectly! They catch it from honest parents who are seeking to have a relationship with God in the midst of the roller coaster of life. This is much more attractive and desirable than parental machines who repeat scripted prayers or pray only at prescribed times. Kids with parents who demand that you *must* have a quiet time every day at a certain time in a particular location for a specific length of time are not likely to thrive under that kind of rigidity. Who wants to be a spiritual robot? People typically resist that kind of spirituality because it looks more like being in the military than being in a loving relationship with the Savior. Your children certainly will reject it. It is better to be *drawn* into any of the spiritual disciplines than pushed.

Successful parents are those who take prayer and its practice *very* seriously and have a regular time of quietness with the Lord. But they also do so in the reality and flow of regular life. Successful parents are those who model prayer in "nonofficial" situations, in the midst of life. Pray for safety in the car. Certainly over meals. Pray for friends—right then and there—who you learn are sick or having difficulty. Pray for the neighbors when you learn they are having particular troubles or a big event coming up. Ask your children if there are needs or struggles their own friends are having that you can offer up to God. This can be very attractive and will have a profound impact on our kids if done in genuine sincerity.

Make prayer more than requests as well, as important as those might be. Offer brief and sincere prayers of thanks and praise for the beautiful sunset emerging before you, for how good the freshly cut grass smells, for how happy your dog seems. Our Father delights in hearing His children get excited about what we are experiencing, just as we delight in our own children doing the same thing. Who is not moved with total joy when your kids run ahead of you on a walk and yell, "Dad, look at these butterflies! I want to catch one!" Our heavenly Father is the same. So feel free to be that kind of child with our Father in the presence of your own children. It will make a difference.

You can also make your prayers simple exclamations. Sometimes, even with your eyes open, if you dare. "Lord, please comfort and heal those people injured in that automobile accident. Comfort their families and be with the EMTs." Praying such prayers from time to time teaches your children that you are—and they can become—regularly aware of God's presence in what you are experiencing in daily life. And the impromptu and "casualness" of these prayers communicates your comfort and security in God as our Father. Our kids will naturally pick up these messages, and they are massively important and powerful. Who wouldn't be drawn to a faith like that? Formal prayers are very helpful and important as well, such as those at mealtime and the recited prayers like the Lord's Prayer or praying the Psalms. Demonstrate to your kids that there are many types of prayer, and God delights in them all.

Your children are not just learning about prayer, but about your own relationship and intimacy with Christ when they hear you pray from your heart. Think of those who have influenced you through their prayers. Learn from and follow some of those examples.

2. Reading God's Word

The research also consistently finds, not surprisingly, that kids who learn to make reading, studying, meditating upon, and practically applying Scriptures a natural part of their lives are kids who will take those practices into adulthood with them. They learn the wisdom, insight, encouragement, correction, comfort, and spiritual growth the Scriptures bring makes for a happier life.

But like prayer, reading the Word cannot be taught as a burden that *must* be done every day or else. I remember the father of one of my friends who was like this, a Scripture-reading and praying taskmaster. He was hard on his kids if they didn't maintain the same discipline. I remember thinking, even as a young teenager, that I might rather take my chances with God than face the wrath of this father if I were to miss a day. Guess what? His son didn't take up the practice of loving to read the Bible.

Demonstrate for your kids that you gain lots of different gems from Scripture and help them learn to do the same for themselves. They can study it as serious, junior-theologians, learning about God and His world. They can study it for its encouragement as well as correction. They can study it for its history of God's redemptive plan. They can read it for its sheer beauty, for it is a gift of God's very word to each of us. They can read it for simple enjoyment. Help them learn to reverence it. Help them learn in real life ways that just as we need actual bread to live, we also need to hear from God through His Word, as Jesus Himself tells us (Matthew 4:4).

Besides the actual activity of reading the Scriptures together, talk about things you've read from the Scriptures throughout the day, when driving to ball practice, when raking leaves, when lying out in the backyard under the tree. As they get older, ask your kids for their insights on the Scriptures you have read and really be interested in their thoughts. This will demonstrate to them that you are coming to trust and welcome their growing insight and spiritual maturity. You might be surprised and strengthened by what you hear. What kid is not going to take that as a great encouragement, even wanting to be ready the next time you might ask?

These are just a few ways parents can sink the love of searching the Scriptures into their kids without them even realizing it. Make it a part of your everyday life, "when you sit in your house, and when you walk by the way, and when you lie down, and when you rise," as we are told in Deuteronomy 6:7. Integrate it naturally into your life together, helping your kids feel it as a natural part of what it means to be a Smith, Jones, Hanson, or McKee. It is what you as a particular family of people do.

3. Faith Experiences in Daily Life

The third most foundational practice is learning to see and experience God working in our everyday lives. This includes things like regular prayer and Bible reading, as we just saw, but also being a part of a good, vibrant Bible-teaching and faith-practicing church, and participating in the work and ministry of that church. It's serving others with acts of kindness, knowing that our faith calls us to such things. These can be simple acts, like helping a neighbor unload groceries or lending them your lawnmower. Essentially, it's getting into the mindset of regularly asking, "Who can I be a blessing to today?" and doing it. A faith that is regularly given away is also a faith that tends to stick to where it came from as well.

Being mindful of God in our daily lives includes praying faithfully for something needed and watching God provide: finances for the family's necessities, the health of a family member or friend, getting a job after being laid off, the salvation of a loved one. Participating in such prayers builds faith in us as well as our children. These experiences accumulate piece by piece, bit by bit, many small stones collected over time making a strong and lasting fortress of faith within them. To use another metaphor, being regularly active in such things is what will drive the practice of spiritual life and actions into the very fibers of our children's DNA. Their faith will become a part of who they are, and "who they are" will remain who they are in adulthood.

Help your children find the activities that meld with their growing personality, desires, and gifts. You might be very big on memorizing Scripture, and your child might be big on serving others. Let your child become and be the individual God created him or her to be.

This developing independence will make the mortar between these bricks hold stronger and longer because these activities have become distinctly *theirs*.

4. Experiencing Miracles

Related to daily prayer, regular Bible reading, and faith experiences is the importance of experiencing miracles, the clear, unmistakable hand of God in our lives. Who will not learn to walk more closely with God when they see Him do unbelievable things? Of course this has a profound impact, as the cold, calculated scientists of Christian Smith's research team found out. Some of us as Christians see genuine miracles more often than others. Some may have never seen them. Those who think they never see miracles need to learn to see them, as they happen all around us much more often than we imagine. We must have eyes to see and ears to hear, as Jesus tells us. We should all see and experience them from time to time because we serve a miraculous God. However, we must take the seeking-out and recognition of such miracles seriously. Don't be the mom who prays for a parking spot close to the door of the supermarket and shouts, "It's a miracle! Praise Jesus!" when she finds one. The only things your kids will learn from this is that their mom or dad is a flake. Ha!

Take God seriously. Read about miracles in the Scriptures. Talk about them as a family. Read stories from ancient and recent church history about the saints who've experienced miracles. Let your children experience how God works, sometimes in very simple ways, but also in profound ways. However, nothing can shore up one's faith like experiencing genuine miracles for oneself. And they don't have to be "raised from the dead" or a "limbs that grow back" kinds of miracles, although these certainly happen. They can be more "regular" miracles, such as praying and seeing your family get the money you need for tomorrow's bills or Aunt Judy's cancer going away when the doctors gave her a dire diagnosis. Our kids will also see that not all prayers get answered and that can be disappointing. But some do, and only in ways that can be described as miraculous. When you hear of this happening with close friends or extended family, share those stories with your children with praise and excitement.

When we encourage our kids in word and deed to be bold in our requests to God and petition Him for the unexpected or impossible and God does what God is so good at doing, those experiences stick with them for life in mighty ways. It is difficult to one day turn your back on a God who is clearly supernatural, powerful, and has shown Himself delighted in meeting your needs. These experiences also become very strong mortar in the brick wall of faith in Christ that you are building in your children.

5. Resolving Doubts

Doubts can actually make our children's faith stronger. How in the world can that be true?

Kids who are able to be honest about their faith doubts and dilemmas, who are encouraged to wrestle honestly with them and seek out solid answers, become kids who are very likely to hang on to their faith. Parents are the first source and greatest help in providing the environment for this. Encourage your kids to be honest about their doubts and questions, both big and small. Share some of your own in age-appropriate ways. Help them wrestle with and work to overcome their own. It is all right and maybe even better if this takes a little while to work these doubts and struggles out. Some of the bigger questions require time to resolve. Sometimes we must give our children the answers to their questions immediately. Other times we have to walk through them together. We should also help them discover where to find the answers for themselves. The "teach a man to fish" thing.

If you are always giving your kids the answers to their spiritual doubts and concerns, they are not learning to dig, ask the right questions, and explore for themselves. And like anything else in life, if they don't master doing this well as they grow into their teen years, they will not be able to do it in their young adult years. They will have to keep coming back home to get their spiritual shoelaces tied, and that's no way to live.

I had a childhood friend who, at age sixteen, said he could no longer believe in God because of all the evil in the world. How could a loving God permit such things? Rather than freaking out, his parents kept a cool head. First, they talked this out with their son, asking him questions about his new conviction. They let him explain and then explored the fullness of that line of thinking with him, to the point of seeming to endorse it themselves. Of course they didn't, but they were supporting their son's thinking process—not his conclusions—by explaining that such concerns were indeed reasonable. They told him many Christians and nonbelievers have struggled with such concerns since ancient days and he was not being rebellious for doing so.

What my friend learned, and what I gleaned by watching it up close, was that asking tough questions and even having doubts about our faith wasn't being unfaithful. It was a natural part of growing up and working to own one's faith, pushing on it some to see if it stands up to the test. My friend's struggle showed that he was thinking seriously about his faith, something that was good and mature. But in the way his parents handled this, they gained the trust of their son because they took his concerns seriously without dismissing or slapping them down. And it was upon this foundation of respect that they were gently and carefully able to talk to him about his doubts over the next few months, providing possible answers and things for him to think about from very smart, experienced Christian thinkers who had found solid answers to the same doubt. My buddy's parents had no idea that their approach had a profound impact on me as I heard about it through him. Your children will certainly not be the only beneficiaries of your work in all of these areas.

My friend eventually came to realize that his reason for rejecting his belief in God was not so well founded. It just sounded sophisticated. He came to understand that evil does exist, not because God is not powerful or that He doesn't care, but because He gives us the choice of whether we want to love and be obedient to Him or go our own way, living by our own rules. True love never forces others to give it.

As well, and most wonderfully, he came to see that it was the cross itself that helped him overcome his problem of doubt. His parents didn't give him this powerful insight. God gave it to him. The death of God's own Son on the cross was a grave evil, and God permitted it so that evil and the evil one could be struck down for good and we would no longer need to live in bondage to it or under its pain. Pain and loss were a mysterious but real part of God's own life. My friend learned that God had made a wonderful way of hope through the things that seemed like roadblocks. And He did so through the terrible sacrifice of His own Son. My buddy's faith grew stronger because of this process. That would not have happened had his parents simply said, "Well, that's wrong. We will pray for you to know the truth."

6. Persecution

Another counterintuitive aspect that strengthens our children's faith is experiencing persecution. Researchers explain that things like committing to virginity, being pro-life, or sharing the gospel with friends at school are all important, and not just because of the benefits of the thing itself. Doing things for our faith that cut against the grain of their community requires something of our kids. They will wrestle with, "Is it really worth it to be made fun of or seem like a freak?" Like struggling with their own doubts, they are learning to own their faith and decide whether it is true enough to get some grief for it. Just as muscles grow stronger and bigger with the resistance provided by lifting weights and doing push-ups, so does our faith.

7. Satellite Adults

When our kids were in the middle of their teen years, we saw something very surprising, remarkable, and totally unexpected happen with each of them. We saw them getting spiritual encouragement and teaching from other adults, and we saw them growing tremendously from it. Up to that time, the only people who influenced them were their mom and me. But that all changed at a certain point in their lives. It was really quite striking. It really started with the couple that led our church's youth group. We saw the very meaningful impact they were having on our kids. And much of it came from just them being them.

We also started to see how their friends' parents, adult Young Life leaders, and even teachers were having a deep impact on their spiritual maturity and growth. Even their maternal grandmother, a woman with a very simple but enticing faith, and aunts and uncles became spiritual mentors to them in more substantive, grown-up ways. We would hear them talking about some spiritual truth they learned or an experience they had through one of these other relationships. It was encouraging to discover we had good spiritual helpers coming alongside us. It's likely these people never realized the impact they were having on our kids. But we could see it so clearly. And we have been so deeply thankful to each of them. Now our kids have become the same kinds of influence on other younger kids. It's a really wonderful thing to see.

The experts call these important people either "scaffolding" or "satellite" adults. *Scaffolding* because they're important and trusted adults who come up alongside our children to build them up and strengthen them. *Satellites* because they are regularly orbiting them during everyday life, watching them, sending and receiving important messages back and forth. Sometimes they are not even noticed by our children, but they are there having a very real influence none-theless. They are trusted and dependable adults who function like additional parents, but in some uniquely influential ways.

These players in our kids' spiritual development are far more important than they realize. When you tell them about their impact, they will usually respond, "I'm not really doing anything important. Just being their friend, being there for them, someone safe to confide in when they need it." *Just?* This role is huge for kids in their teens and early adult years, an absolute treasure for their spiritual and emotional development. The reasons why are not difficult to figure out.

First, as we have seen in ample detail, kids learn their faith from parents who practice a serious faith. But, as we all know, parents can be squares, nerds, dups, whatever word every new generation invents to describe them. This has always been the case as long as people have been making the transition from childhood into adult-hood. But when other adults who are not squares, nerds, dups, et cetera, come along and back up what Mom and Dad have been saying for years, that is spiritual money in the bank when it comes to building faith on our kids. "Sure, Mom and Dad have told me all these things about God, and I love them dearly. But sometimes they just don't know." But when our children experience other adults who share your values and faith, they come to this conclusion: "But Bethany, a volunteer in my youth group who rides a motorcycle, is also very committed to Christ too. And she shows me different sides of faith that I have never seen from my parents. Maybe there is really something to all of this!" When the cool adults who "get it" back up

Mom and Dad, maybe Mom and Dad aren't so dumb after all, right?

Also, our children are likely to feel more comfortable being honest and transparent about their questions and struggles around such adults. They are adults, but they're not their parents. It is extremely valuable for your kids to have trusted adults in their lives that they look up to but whose beliefs, values, and convictions are also in line with yours. In many ways these people are serving as the first concentric circle of influencers, encouragers, and protectors around your children. They have your back as well as the back of your child, and they help span that natural parent/child gap that maturity brings.

And they don't always have to be cool either. They just have to be wise and sincere, making it clear they care deeply for your child. Think about who these people were in your own childhood. Did you have a teacher, family member, or friend whom you respected, trusted, and confided in? They may not have had an ounce of hipness in them, but that didn't matter. You knew they had wisdom, could be trusted, and cared for you deeply. As such, they were likely one of the most transformative people in your young life. Work to make sure your child grows up with at least one or two of these satellite adults around them. Go looking for and recruiting them if you have to. Be responsive when other parents come to you for the same help.

* * *

These seven experiences and qualities are the primary things researchers find present in the lives and practices of parents who are successfully passing on their faith to their children and who have these children grow into adulthood with a living and lasting faith. Having as many of these as possible be a part of your children's lives will dramatically boost your children's chances of taking a maturing faith into adulthood with them and passing it on to your grandchildren. To summarize, parents whose children retain and grow in their faith

1. take their faith very seriously and live it out in meaningful ways;
2. exhibit relational warmth toward their children;
3. help their children develop a serious practice of regular, intimate prayer by modeling it, not forcing it;
4. instill a love for and practice of reading the Scriptures regularly by doing so themselves;
5. encourage the participation of various regular religious practices—beyond prayer and Scripture reading—like regular church attendance; serving others by teaching Sunday school class; volunteering in the nursery; feeding, clothing, and caring for the poor; raising money for ministries they are passionate about, and the like—essentially just getting involved in things that serve others because of their faith;
6. help their children experience and take note of miracles in their own lives and the lives of others;
7. help their children be honest about and resolve their own spiritual doubts and struggles;
8. help their children stand strong in the face of persecution

    from peers and teachers due to their moral and faith con-
    victions that seem unpopular;

9. help and encourage their children in developing relation-
    ships with satellite adults who are trusted and share your
    family's faith and convictions.

You can fail at all the other things you feel one is supposed to do as a successful Christian parent and not lose the game. But succeed *moderately well* at most of these things we've explored above, and the best, most careful, rigorous research from leading scholars tells us your kids will be *extremely* likely to develop and hang on to a beautiful, living, and lasting faith into their adult lives.

The great news is that none of these things are really rocket science. They can be done by anyone regardless of their level of education, financial resources, where they live, or even their spiritual maturity. No one is excluded or more qualified than another at doing any of them. The honesty, sincerity, and passion of your own heart is what will really make you successful. Your kids want to know if these things are real within you, whether you really take them seriously or not, even if you don't always live them out perfectly. If they do see these things in you, their faith is very likely to stick.

This, parents, is very good news! The process is not that difficult, but the results are eternal. And the likelihood of your efforts being successful is very high. Take great comfort and encouragement in these facts. God would not make such essential developments in our children so complicated that it would be unlikely we could accomplish them. He knows how inadequate we are in that task. That is why, just like we all tell our kids, Jesus shows us what to do and tells us, "Just do your best and you'll be fine."

God is a very gracious Father who desires our children's hearts and spiritual well-being far more than we ever could. He just wants us to partner with Him in doing this significant work.

CHAPTER 9

"IS MY CHURCH SHRINKING?" AND OTHER QUESTIONS TO CONSIDER

We have seen a very compelling case that the church is not going up in flames, imploding, shrinking to nothing, sinking to the depths of the ocean, or being sucked into a black hole. The undertaker has not been called, and the fat lady has not even thought about her sheet music. But did we really need so much research to tell us this? It is certainly helpful, and it girds up our confidence in the facts and stokes our encouragement in the future of the church. That is all good and essential.

But while the Chicken Littles do all their squawking, can't we just look around and figure out what's true by observing the state of churches we see every day? Ask yourself these questions:

- Are churches being boarded up where you live, having "everything must go" liquidation sales?
- How many churches do you know of that had to move to smaller facilities because of shrinking crowds?
- How many pastors do you know who are now on unemployment or selling insurance because their churches evaporated?
- How many churches do you know that once had a thriving youth ministry, but now only have a part-time youth pastor and a smattering of kids? If the accepted narrative is true about youth and the church, shouldn't there be thousands of once-upon-a-time youth pastors now selling cell phones at a kiosk in the mall or delivering pizzas? How many do you know of who have lost their job because of dwindling crowds?

Your own real-life experiences and observations are not scientific like the rest of the data we have studied, but they can be very informative nonetheless. Is your church shrinking? Are your friends' churches declining? What about the churches you pass every day on your way to your kids' schools, to the grocery store, to work, or the bank? How are those churches doing? We see businesses shutting down and boarded up all the time, but we never really say, "Retail is dying!" How many of us have been laid off from our jobs in the last ten years? It's what happens and few people are going all Chicken Little.

But this is *not* what we are seeing in the churches in our neighborhoods. But because we hear so many gloom and doom stories, we assume it must be happening elsewhere. It's really not, though. Your community is not really that different than any other a thousand miles away. So why do we accept the Chicken Little narrative when few of us have ever seen any actual real-life evidence of it in our communities? It is a very good question to ask those spreading the false news. In this chapter we will see that churches are actually one of the most stable and consistent community institutions in any town.

Let's look at a few key measures or indicators of the vitality of the church today that make a positive case for the general well-being and even growing vitality of the church in the early twenty-first century. Like many things we see every day as a normal part of our lives, they are so "regular" and constant we tend not to notice them at all. Hopefully looking at some additional key real-life indicators will cause us to ask ourselves the question, "How could I have ever believed the church was dying without looking around me to see what is actually happening in my own community and those I have visited?"

Imagine this. You're *much* older and your *great*-grandkids ask you, "Great-grandpa/grammy, what were churches like when you were young?" You could tell those sweet kids each of the following things, and they would all most likely be true of your experience:

- If you drove anywhere, in short distances, you would pass at least two or three churches. Oftentimes they had these catchy little sayings on their signs out front like "Ch_ _ ch. What's Missing? UR." Many were cornier than a bag of Doritos, but they were fun to read. Lots of churches had these. You couldn't escape them.

- In the summer you could pass by these churches and they would have creative and colorful signs by the road advertising something called Vacation Bible Schools. Kids could nearly fill up every week of their summer by going from one VBS to another, there were so many in any decent-sized town.

- There were these things called "megachurches," and they called them this because thousands of people attended them every week. They were like concert halls or sports stadiums. They were huge! In fact, they often had two or three services on Sunday, even Saturday night, to make space for all the folks who came. The doors were never locked from morning till late evening during the week because something was *always* going on there.

- Many of these churches had so many attending that they had to hire off-duty police officers to direct traffic in and out of the parking lots each Sunday. It was really quite something to see.

- There were groups like Awana and Young Life for kids, special groups where elementary, middle, and high school kids could meet each week to have fun together and grow in their faith. Those groups were pretty big, and you could find something similar at most churches. In fact, these churches hired full-time pastors just to work with the kids, and some of these groups had hundreds of kids participating.

- Every summer tens of thousands of kids from churches across the country went on mission trips to serve people in some poorer part of our own nation or in another country. They went to inner cities to clean up and beautify playgrounds, to Native American reservations to teach children, to third-world countries to build schools or dig wells. Kids saved up or held car washes to earn money for these trips. Some of us even got a little tired of so many kids asking for donations each spring to send them on these trips, which were quite popular.

- In the largest stores like Walmart and Target, grocery stores, and even airports, you would easily find shelves of Christian books to buy and they sold quite well.

- You could go to coffee shops and very likely find young adults from local churches holding a Bible study there or find one teenager just reading the Scriptures or some popular Christian book.

- Christian music for young people was very popular, and every year there were new artists hitting the charts—that's what we called it back in the day—who were unknown the previous year. Many of the most popular worship songs were sung in local churches.

- You could easily find massive Christian conferences around the country to go to. These would be for young people, families, church staff, some just for women, and others just for men. Oftentimes, the difficulty was deciding which ones to go to because few had the time and money to attend them all. Most denominations would have huge summer conferences that would take up whole convention centers in some of our nation's largest cities.

- Parents associated with local churches would start new Christian schools in their communities to provide their children with a strong Christian education. Christian colleges were scattered across the nation so young people could get a good education in a Christian atmosphere. Most of them grew nicely, even the small ones, regularly adding beautiful new buildings to their campuses. Many provided convenient, growing, online classes for students who couldn't actually attend their campus. These were very popular.

- In most cities there were Christian radio stations that played really wonderful praise music. They also had teaching from some of the world's best Christian pastors, writers, and speakers. These stations were very popular among people who attended church, and there was really nowhere you could drive in America and not be able to easily find at least one on the radio.

- While not as numerous, you could also find whole television networks of Christian teaching and programming nearly anywhere in the United States and around the world.

- There were also countless Christian podcasts that young people would listen to on their phones, and their numbers and audiences grew each year. Many of these podcasts contained pastors' sermons so church members could always keep up with what was going on even if they missed church for any reason, or they could "attend" other churches while driving in their car by listening to a pastor from another church. It was as if folks didn't want to find themselves anywhere where they could not easily access good Christian teaching.

- Young adult couples and individuals would regularly make appointments with fellow believers to sit down and ask if they would be willing to support them as full-time missionaries in some part of the world. Sometimes they would be doing ministry work right in their own country. But nearly any Christian who regularly attended church over the years would be asked by some young person for this kind of help at some point.

Anyone who pays the slightest bit of attention to church culture knows each of these are true today and exist in every town of any considerable size. They are what we call "common." And here is the best news. They will also be common in the world those great-grandkids will grow up in and even new ways of practicing and proclaiming the faith to even more people will become common as well. The best sociologists of religion have no doubt that it will. God's kingdom cannot *not* grow and advance. It's what it does.

A robust and complex study was published in the *Journal for the*

Scientific Study of Religion on how many churches in the United States die every year. It's a remarkable article and what they found was nothing short of stunning. Get this. Only 1 percent of church congregations in the United States die every year! The authors of this article explain this is an "unusually low" close rate for *any type* of organization in a community. The average close rate for a community organization is about 5 percent or higher annually. The only organization these researchers could find that came close to the church's 1 percent close rate were childcare centers. But not just any centers. They could find a comparably low annual close rate only for those in Toronto, Canada. That's it. They had to find that tiny needle in the haystack for anything that came close.[1] They were not able to find any kind of larger community organization that rivaled the sustained success and longevity of churches. If you were an investor putting your money into community organizations, this is one group you and all your peers would be investing in with great frequency and confidence. Your colleagues would call you a fool if you didn't.

On top of this, let's survey the numbers for a few key growth indicators for Christian practice and ministry over the past few years and decades. And let me be honest with you. I didn't look for those that were positive and avoid the negative. As I was laying out this chapter, I began by simply making a list of the main parts and components that make up overall Christian ministry in a community and then looked at research from the best sources I could find to see what story it told. I was really quite surprised by what I found. I think you will be too.

YOUTH MINISTRY

One of the best representational youth ministries both in the United States and globally is Young Life. They work with students in middle school, high school, and college, and have done so since 1941. If it were true that young people have been leaving the Christian church in droves, how has Young Life fared over this period of time? Their vital numbers absolutely surprised me.

In the past ten years, this ministry has seen constant and sustained growth in terms of number of kids involved and reached; number of staff, volunteers, and local group leaders; and annual income. In fact, every one of their key ministry indicators has increased overall since their founding, right up to the present day. Nothing but sustained growth. Let's look at some specifics.[2]

First, let's look at what's been happening in Young Life's weekly clubs. These are weekly gatherings that happen in a particular school or community. From 2009 to 2017, youth attendance at these meetings in the United States increased 31 percent. Internationally, attendance increased 416 percent! Four. Hundred. Sixteen. Kids are interested.

Young Life's Campaigners are more serious weekly gatherings where kids learn how to grow in their faith through Bible study, service to others, and developing leadership skills. From 2009 to 2017, weekly attendance for these groups in the US increased 69 percent and an incredible 620 percent internationally! Remember in a previous chapter when Professor Jenkins used the word *booming* to describe the growth he was seeing in Christianity in many parts of the world? A 620 percent increase might justify upgrading that superlative to *exploding*.

Schools reached and impacted by Young Life groups as well as all their other ministries in the US and internationally increased 73 percent overall from 2009 to 2017. The number of volunteer leaders, both youth and adults, increased 94 percent in the United States and a whopping 265 percent internationally.

Does this seem like teens are developing dramatically less interest in Christianity? Ask youth workers in Young Life and other youth ministries what they're seeing. They probably won't report all-out revival, but that's not the case this book is seeking to make. Not at all. I'm only seeking to prove that young people and adults are *not* abandoning the church, leaving Christ's bride with a very grim future. Instead, robust growth is happening.

How about for young adults attending college? Certainly the secularizing effects of academia are dousing students' interest in spiritual matters. That's a very steady and unquestioned assumption among Christians and others. Let's see if that's true.

SECULAR COLLEGE CAMPUSES

Like Young Life for middle and high school kids, InterVarsity is a flagship ministry in evangelicalism that reaches out to college students on secular campuses, large and small, across the country. Their most recent annual reports show that the overall number of chapters on college campuses has grown 14 percent over the past five years. That number is simply continuing the considerable growth they've seen *every* year since the organization's founding in 1941. They have 1,015 chapters today on 687 campuses, the most they have ever had. The number of students and faculty involved in InterVarsity small groups is up 35 percent over ten years ago. Involvement of international students in IV's US chapters is up 26 percent over that same time. Graduate student involvement is up 9 percent over the last ten years, and more faculty members are involved in IV groups than ever before, 48 percent more than in 2007. That's nothing short of stunning.

Looking at these numbers it would be hard to say college campuses and faculty are secular wastelands devoid of any vibrant Christian influence. The number of people who have made decisions to become Christians through InterVarsity outreaches increased 36 percent over the last five years. In 2017, they reached their *highest number of new Christians ever*. That's a 12 percent increase over 2015 and a 130 percent increase in decisions for Christ since 2007. Let's pay close attention to this. InterVarsity's heyday for decisions for Christ was not in what many would claim as the "good ol' days," of the 1940s, '50s, or '60s. Their best days are today, and every indication is they will continue to get better!

On top of this, the ethnic diversity in chapters parallels that of the average ethnic makeup of US universities and colleges. In the last ten years, IV saw 133 percent growth in the number of African American students and faculty involved, a 230 percent increase in Native American involvement, 171 percent increase in Latino Americans, and 48 percent growth in Asian American students and faculty.[3]

These numbers were far stronger than I had anticipated. I had assumed they might simply be flat or show a very slight decline. I was wrong.

CHRISTIAN SCHOOLS AND COLLEGES

Research done jointly at Harvard and Stanford Universities explains that over the last twenty-five years in the United States, the number of specifically conservative Christian elementary schools increased on average by 5 percent, and the number of students attending these schools increased by 9 percent.[4]

In late 2017, *U.S. News and World Report* found that experts were reporting that young adults were choosing distinctly Christian colleges at increasing rates. According to the Council for Christian Colleges and Universities, such schools experienced 17 percent growth in first-time, full-time enrollment from 2003 to 2015.[5] Note that this happened when overall college and university student enrollment declined by 3 percent.[6] That is nothing but positively stunning.

In fact, one of today's most respected and celebrated historians of recent Christian belief and practice, George Marsden, recently wrote a very detailed essay on what he refers to as "a renaissance of Christian higher education in the United States."[7] He says Christian universities are not only getting larger and more numerous today, but *better* academically and in their larger influence upon the world.

Outside of North America, Christian colleges, universities, and seminaries are experiencing even greater growth. One major book-length study on the growth of such institutions around the world noted that 187 new distinctly Christian universities were founded outside North America since 1980, and 138 of those came along since 1990. The hotspots have been throughout Africa, where 46 new Christian universities were birthed between 1990 and 2010.[8] More Christian universities have sprouted up there over the past decade than in all the rest of the world combined! And there are now more Lutheran and Presbyterian universities in Latin America than in all of Europe. These numbers indicate a whole lot of young people seeking out a distinctly Christian education. How could this possibly be if they are leaving that very faith in a mass exodus?

GROWTH OF CHRISTIAN MEDIA AND PUBLISHING

Christians seeking faith-based content from radio, television, and the internet increased 22 percent around the world from 2000 to 2017.[9] What about reading materials for Christians? In a supposedly shrinking church culture and an overall declining publishing market, how are Christian books doing? This will surprise you greatly as well.

- The Association of American Publishers reports that religious book presses grew by 6.9 percent from 2015 to 2016. The overwhelming majority of these are Christian publishers.[10]
- *Publishers Weekly*, the leading trade publication in the book publishing world, reported in 2017 that while overall book industry sales declined by 5 percent between 2015 and 2016, religious titles were one of the strongest growing sectors, with an increase of 7 percent over that year.[11]
- An executive from HarperCollins, a massive global publisher putting out many distinct categories of books, told *Publishers Weekly* that its Christian division was one of their two *strongest* growing divisions in sales for 2018.[12]

- Jim Milliot, a senior writer at *Publishers Weekly*, explained to me that overall, Christian books sales have remained relatively stable in a struggling market. Some Christian publishing houses are doing "very well," in Milliot's words, with what they call "heartland" readers, those living in the flyover country of the United States.
- According to Gordon-Conwell Seminary's Center for the Study of Global Christianity, the number of Christian book titles sold internationally increased 83 percent from 2000 to 2017.
- The number of Bibles printed and distributed internationally increased 63 percent from 2000 to 2017. Given the costs of printing and transporting such a relatively large book, they are certainly only being printed according to demand.

DENOMINATIONAL GROWTH

According to the Center for the Study of Global Christianity at Gordon-Conwell Theological Seminary, from 2000 to 2017, the Christian denominations or tradition groups listed below *grew* by the following percentages worldwide:

- Evangelicals: 43 percent
- Pentecostal/Charismatic: 45 percent
- Independent churches: 45 percent
- Protestants (in general): 32 percent
- Roman Catholic: 20 percent[13]

We must recognize something very important here regarding the last two traditions on this list. As we saw clearly in previous chapters, the more liberal and lukewarm sectors of the church are the ones declining in terms of congregations as a whole as well as in individual attendees. Therefore, any growth among general Protestant and Roman Catholic churches would indicate that growth is coming from increasing conservative clergy and attendees. When we consider these two 32 and 20 percent growth rates since 2000, we must take into account that conservatives have most certainly filled the massive hole left by the exiting liberals and lukewarms, *and* on top of this, added even more to reflect such overall growth. That's like measuring your child's height and seeing notable growth even though you made her stand in a hole as you measured her. The numbers regarding Protestant and Catholic growth are remarkable by any standard.

MISSIONARY EFFORTS

What about efforts to grow the church, to go into all the world and make disciples of all nations? Are the numbers of people willing to do such difficult work shrinking or growing? Aren't missionaries something from a passed age? If the church is shrinking, surely the number of missionaries is shrinking as well. Let's look at additional 2018 information from Gordon-Conwell's Center for the Study of Global Christianity.

- Foreign Christian missionaries increased overall by 2 percent from 2000 to 2017. This is certainly not a news-making increase, but it's not a decline either.

- Missionary-sending organizations increased by 33 percent around the world from 2000 to 2017.
- Non-Christians around the world who know someone who is a Christian increased 4 percent from 2000 to 2017. This means more people around the world have the opportunity to hear the gospel and see the Christian life demonstrated in real, everyday life from someone they have a personal relationship with.
- The percentage of the world's population that has no opportunity to hear the gospel decreased 5 percent from 2000 to 2017.[14]

CHRISTIAN GIVING

In a world where very few things happen without money, we must examine how financial giving to Christian causes is doing in recent years. Again, surprising findings!

- Giving to local churches alone internationally increased 177 percent from 2000 to 2017, presently at $360 billion. (Yes, that's a *b*!)
- Giving to parachurch organizations around the world increased 184 percent from 2000 to 2017, presently at $540 billion.
- Income for all foreign global missions increased 194 percent from 2000 to 2017, presently at $53 billion.
- Total giving to Christian work internationally increased 181 percent from 2000 to 2017, presently at $900 billion.

People don't tend to give increasing amounts of their hard-earned money to a movement that's tanking. In fund-raising, success breeds success and that is certainly the case in philanthropy toward the church.

CHURCH CONSTRUCTION

Earlier in this chapter we learned that sophisticated university research has found that only 1 percent of churches die in any given year. But what about new ones? Are new churches springing up in the United States or is construction declining or merely remaining flat? No one builds new churches for seriously declining crowds.

A recent article published in the *Journal for the Scientific Study of Religion* presenting research conducted at Duke University improves upon how we count the number of congregations in America. The author concludes that there has most likely been an increase overall in congregations—and thus the buildings that house them—over the last ten to fifteen years, even accounting for the decline of the most liberal congregations. The nondenominational churches have been, far and away, the ones accounting for this growth, with an increase of 56 percent from 1998 to 2012.[15]

One church construction business in rural Georgia says that despite the naysayers in the press, their business has been booming. They observed in their Southern, homespun way that "you can't throw a rock around here without hitting a church building, and that's part of why we love living and building here." Their business is brisk and growing. They add that these are not dinosaur churches either. "What's more, our church communities aren't simply older generations holding on to a forgotten past. . . . In Macon they are young, vibrant, and growing."

A 2018 article in the *Religious Product News* on construction trends of local churches opens with this recognition:

Church design and construction has become a multibillion-dollar industry. While it used to be big news that a local church had broken ground on a new facility, today it is difficult to drive through a city without seeing multiple church building projects under construction.

Notice two important words used in this statement: *has become.* And what "has become" refers to *a multibillion-dollar industry.* The writer did not say "used to be" or "is likely to never become" but used the definitive *has become* to describe a massively lucrative industry.

Google the phrase "trends in church construction" and you will immediately see that this is a very vibrant and growing industry. You will see many sites explaining and offering resources for the emerging creative trends in church constructions. You will be struck by the fresh creativity, innovation and technical sophistication of this growing multibillion-dollar industry. It is clearly not in decline in any way. Dying industries don't tend to put out annual updates on what exciting new designs and trends are *not* coming next year. New churches being built today are getting increasingly creative and diverse in design, and are multiuse. *Multiuse.* Meaning, "There are many more activities going on at our church, so we have to make creative use of space." It's a good and significant problem that more and more churches are having to deal with.

MEGACHURCHES

Finally, the big daddies that the Chicken Littles are all aware of—who can miss them?—but seem to ignore what they really are at the same time: *megachurches*.

Consider that prefix *mega*. It means more than big. It's MEGA. The Big Gulp or the Mega Gulp of Mountain Dew? One will serve you well if you're *really* thirsty. The other will serve you *very* well if you have a double shift at work; it may even make you feel you could pull a triple. Would you like a *huge* stack of free twenty dollar bills or the *mega* stack? Mega, please.

We know these megachurches are quite plentiful, and they have arisen only in the last thirty years. If you live in a decent-sized city, you likely have at least one and probably more in your town. Think about that. These giants are springing up at a time when the church is supposed to be disappearing. That's what we call ironic.

A cooperative effort between the Leadership Network and the Hartford Institute for Religious Research at Hartford Seminary in Connecticut conducted an in-depth examination of the growth and health of megachurches. What they found was extremely interesting and important.

The average megachurch has roughly two thousand or more people attending each weekend! The largest have as many as thirty thousand people in their services every week. Megachurches have an average of five different services every weekend to accommodate all those who come. Sixty-two percent of these churches are multisite congregations, meaning they have a number of different physical locations around their city and typically simulcast the service from one campus to all the others. The average number of sites for these churches is 3.5 per church, which also makes them more multiracial and culturally diverse than the average church, as these sites are intentionally planted in different neighborhoods around town.

What is most remarkable is megachurches continue to grow at a very steady pace, with thirty-nine churches across the country having grown to "mega" status between 2010 and 2015. Roughly 40 percent of megachurch attendees are part of a small group within their church. Either we are having a massive exodus from the church or substantial growth of megachurches. We can't have both at the same time, and the data is clear as day as to which one is actually happening.

The bare fact is that no other age in church history has experienced the existence of so many churches this large. *None.* The Leadership Network/Hartford Institute research finds that most of these churches continue to grow every year, and often at remarkably fast rates. The numbers speak for themselves. Over a five-year period,

- 12 percent of megachurches increased their average attendance from 2 to 9 percent.
- 39 percent of megachurches increased their average attendance from 10 to 49 percent.
- 19 percent of megachurches increased their average attendance from 50 to 99 percent.

- 13 percent had an increase of 100 percent or higher.
- Only 17 percent experienced any kind of decline, and these are typically not because of a decline of interest among attendees, but because of some moral or leadership crisis in the church.

Some people refer to megachurches as the Walmarts of religion, but that's not a fair assessment. While a Walmart moving into a community unfortunately may put some mom-and-pop shops out of business, we don't see a parallel phenomenon in the church world. Remember the unique 1 percent annual close rate for churches. The megachurches are certainly drawing believers from other smaller churches, but they are not putting them out of business. There seems to be enough growth to go around, which is simply quite remarkable by any measure.

Given this historic trend, the Leadership Network/Hartford Institute Report also shows that 64 percent of megachurches report an increase in *young adults* attending their churches in the past three years. Get that. A sizable majority of these churches see increasing numbers of young people attending and participating at the very time when . . . say it with me . . . "young people are leaving the church in droves." Again, you can have one or the other, but you can't have both.

Most megachurches emphasize young adult programs, and 86 percent say they put a great deal of energy and resources into programs for teenagers. Nearly all megachurch leaders say their programs and outreach to young adults are a main ministry priority.

These researchers explain, "Giving young adult ministry a priority status makes a difference; the more a church is intentional about young adult ministry, the larger percentage of them it will have in the congregation."[16] And that is clearly showing itself true in actual experience.

IS THERE *ANY* BAD NEWS?

In concluding these last eight chapters on the research behind conservative Christianity's very bright and growing present and future, it is important to recognize and admit that there are certainly numbers and reports that draw a negative picture of what is happening in the church today. It's not all roses by any stretch. Biblical literacy seems to be declining in very concerning ways. The church is being increasingly commercialized, marketing to its members as much as ministering to them. There are too many pastors who never say anything hard or demanding from the pulpit. Too many who preach a happy-clappy faith of happiness and prosperity. Yes, bad teaching does exist in the church. There always has, as many of the apostolic epistles in the New Testament deal with correcting bad behavior and problems within the various churches. Yes, all is not peaches and cream.

A negative picture of what's happening with Christianity today in terms of growth and trends can be constructed, to be sure. We have all seen them. But these numbers and examples often come from weak studies drawn from unrepresentative samples or poor methodologies. As we have discussed throughout this book, some data is terribly weak but still gets reported in otherwise reputable papers and magazines. Thus, they take on a seeming sense of strength and authority.

Consider claims like this one that someone asked me about just this week: "*USA Today* reports that 70 percent of young people will leave the faith by the time they reach 18." As we have seen, such a number is nowhere close to reality. But because a major publication says it, it takes on the air of authority and reliability and people use the stat with absolute confidence.

But many will be inclined to ask how so many seemingly reliable sources and reputable ministry leaders could get the story so wrong. It's a very good question worth asking, and it's precisely the one we will take up next.

CHAPTER 10

HOW CAN SMART PEOPLE GET IT SO WRONG?

Every six months, Derek, the youth pastor of a larger-than-average evangelical church in the upper Midwest, hosts a meeting for his parents and volunteers to check up on the status and progress of this ministry in which they all hold a substantial stake. Derek usually starts the meeting with an update on how he thinks the kids are doing collectively as well as some information about trends and concerns in the overall world of youth work. One night he shared a brief online video from a nationally respected youth ministry on how 60 percent of kids in every youth group would arrive at age twenty-one with their faith tossed to the side of the road like an empty soda can. As his assistant hit the pause button on the online clip, Derek laid it out on the table for the parents and staff:

I hope each of you know I'm totally committed to the spiritual care of every one of your kids—more than you can imagine—but given data like this, could it be we are just spinning our wheels? Other than these 40 percent who might stick with their faith, is our collective work failing terribly? Is the church failing? Must we settle for failure, or should we significantly adjust what we are doing, and if so how?

Derek's honest soul-searching set off quite a discussion among the parents. Some were upset at the hint of throwing in the towel, others were greatly shocked and discouraged at such a grim picture, and still others sought to buoy up the group with a declaration of never giving up. This was one of the most discouraging parent meetings Derek had ever overseen. It was also the most discouraged he'd ever been in his ministry.

Derek is certainly not alone. Many in ministry feel the same way given the news they've been told so many times over. This is just one illustration of why we must gain a sure grasp of the truth of what's happening today with the church and stop entertaining and spreading the news of despair, especially when it involves the spiritual well-being and future of our young people.

Parents, you care because these are *your* kids and the dear friends of your kids. Your kids' friends are like your own kids. You've helped raise them in many different ways. If you don't believe this, ask these kids how they feel about you and you will find out what a substantial role you've played in their lives. Think about similar adults in your own life when you were that age. (We addressed the massive significance of such adults in the latter part of chapter 8.) In fact, the spiritual and eternal standing of our children is the most important thing good Christian parents concern themselves with regarding the success and impact of their parenting.

Pastors care deeply about every member of their congregation. They desire that each of us not only hang in there with Christ and His church, but to grow and thrive every year in our relationship with Jesus. It's why they went into this line of work and labor well past quittin' time until all hours of the night. In fact, they have very little actual "off time" because none of us are very good at planning our various crises during regular business hours.

All the bad news of declining faith making the rounds in the church today does not make most Christian workers or parents doubt the importance of their efforts, want to slow down, or determine to give up. Pastors and parents keep at it, with great passion and love. But messages like these do make untold numbers of people like Derek, his volunteers, and the parents of his youth group question whether they are making any real difference. How can it not? It often keeps them up at night, wondering what they are doing wrong and what they should change. Do an online search for "reasons youth are leaving the church" and how to stop it and you will find a month's worth of reading. It seems as if every fourth Christian leader is offering help and reasons for why the decline is happening and what must be done to reverse it. The cottage industry, remember?

What this means of course is that parents and church workers are very busy studying, learning, developing, and practicing new angles and techniques in their work with the hope of staunching the hemorrhage. They are collectively spending millions of dollars each year on materials that promise help in turning around such trends. They do so because according to what they are being told, what they have been doing over the years is obviously not working. In fact, it appears it's making things much worse. The falling sky and all that. We must get on the right side of this story because of a number of important reasons.

- First, it's better to live by truth than falsehood.
- It creates tremendous self-doubt and discouragement in all those who work in the ministry of the church, as either professional staff or volunteers.
- It creates distractions as we seek new and creative ways to gird up faith that we believe is likely to disappear. And these new things don't seem to be working either.
- It can create a kind of self-fulfilling prophecy for our own kids and all the others we work with in our churches and parachurch ministries. Not a few might wonder why they should stick with a faith they are doubting when so many others have supposedly just given up and left. How could so many people be wrong?
- It compels us to spend precious ministry dollars on all the new books, programs, and conferences that promise to fix the problems they warn us about.

If you pay attention, it is usually those who offer us the resources that are the ones citing dire stats, driving a great deal of the "sky is falling" hysteria in the first place. In order to sell your solution, you have to convince your customer of the problem, right?

I am huge fan and advocate of teaching young people and adults Christian apologetics and worldview. Doing so is essential to the life of the church and the defense of the faith. But some of those offering help with apologetics—the very pursuit and explanation of truth—are ironically some of the biggest offenders when it comes to the false Chicken Little narrative. Those offering church-strengthening resources follow close behind.

So, the key question in all of this is: *How can so many smart Christian leaders who truly love and care for the church be so wrong about something so important?*

Well, one reason can be learned from the Chicken Little story itself. Stories of doom spread from one mouth to another ear very efficiently. Something in the human psyche causes us to repeat such tales. One wag correctly said that falsehood will spread throughout the city before the truth has even gotten its pants on. This is why the Chicken Little story has been told to children as a cautionary tale in various ways in many countries and communities since it emerged centuries ago. It is a warning against this "bad news takes swift legs" phenomenon that's common to human culture. It takes boldness, and possible rejection, to stand up and rebuke the fear. But if we are going to exchange a false narrative for a true one, we must know why and how the current one is incorrect. There are a number of reasons for the misunderstandings.

WE'RE NOT THE MISSOURIANS
WE SHOULD BE

Even if we are not from Missouri, we must become like Missourians—those from the Show-Me State. Rather than taking someone's word for it, the show-me-staters want it proven. This is what the Berean Christians did, as we are told in Acts 17:11. They were the original show-me folks. These Jews listened to Paul's teaching with great eagerness, but they searched the Scriptures for themselves to see if what Paul said was actually true. Because of this virtue, the Bereans are described as being "more noble than" others. We must be like them.

Ask for proof and then question the source to see if it's reliable. Just because it appeared in *USA Today* or came from the mouth of a valued leader is not good enough. Trace it to its ultimate source. Too many of us tend to believe whatever we hear someone else say if they say it with confidence. Chicken Little's friends did. But all they had to do was ask C.L. what actually fell from the sky and bopped her on the head. Her friends were not from Missouri. But we should be.

WE PLAY THE TELEPHONE GAME

Another problem that arises quite often here is demonstrated in the telephone game. One source says something that is indeed true, but as the story gets passed from one person to the next, the story changes, and in the end it fails to resemble the original story in any way.

The game is fun because it's human nature to get small details of the story wrong, and it's amusing to find out how crazy the sentence ends up once it made its way around the room. However, when we are dealing with matters of faith, it's not quite so funny to see how distorted the truth can become. When many different people are getting small parts of the story wrong in their own unique and totally innocent way, it can quickly become a very different story.

I come across this when I'm looking at the facts and statistics we want to use in our work at Focus on the Family. A recent example had to do with the power of couples praying together and their reduced risk of divorce. A major marriage ministry stated on their website that research shows—and they cite the original research!—that only 2 percent of couples who pray together will ever get divorced. This would be very good news to share with Christian couples, and it was even based on solid research. We were considering highlighting it ourselves. But it turned out to be wrong. The source itself was indeed a very good study by a respected University of Chicago sociologist. So how could it not be right? Because of the telephone game.

Being the research nerd that I am, I had the book by this sociologist on my shelf so I was able to read it in the original. It's good I did. What this University of Chicago sociologist actually said was that only 2 percent of the couples he surveyed who regularly pray together *believe* they could ever divorce. Do you see the difference here? This statistic didn't say whether they *would* ever get divorced or if they actually did, but rather whether they *believed* that possibility was in their future. A small difference that makes a huge difference. We must always go back to the actual source of the original caller and find out what they actually said if we want to be sure we are quoting material accurately.

WE BELIEVE IN POOR RESEARCH

One of the baseless statistics making the rounds in church circles today with great frequency comes from an extremely well-loved and respected Christian thinker and author. He's a hero of mine. It is said he warned that well over 90 percent of our evangelical youth will not carry their faith into adulthood, or something similar. When he was asked about the statistic, though, he said this number came from an extremely informal poll he did with some youth workers around a lunch table one day at a conference. He well knew and admitted the terribly weak methodology behind the statistic, but it took on a larger, stronger life than it deserved because of the source.

Often statistics arise from research that is decent but not as strong as it should be. The data might seem reputable, but actually involved a telephone survey of one hundred people or so. It might be from a survey distributed and collected at a leadership conference. It might be from a respectable university, but is simply a weak study.

Sometimes the study is conducted by a well-respected Christian research organization or by a reputable scholar with solid methods, but if it is only one study among many, the reader should beware. It is this issue we will address next.

WE HAVE TOO SMALL A VIEW

A very common problem regarding the reporting of stats is having too small a view. A research organization or evangelical university will conduct a research project and come up with noteworthy findings. Sometimes they themselves or other media outlets and Christian leaders will report these finding as the "new normal," as if the current truth on a topic is determined and established by the latest study to come along.

This happens in all kinds of things we discuss in the public square. Are eggs bad for you or not? Is climate change real or not? Is it smart to use hand sanitizer all the time or not? Is wine good for your heart? Does cohabitation contribute to a great risk of divorce or not? Everyone seems to have a different answer, offering their opinion with the same firm confidence and conviction. It all gets so confusing for one simple reason. We make our conclusions based on what was last reported by the media. This is not how good, careful conclusions are made. No real conclusion can be made from simply looking at the last study to come along, but we do it all the time.

One must consider each new study—for good or for bad—against the larger body of research on that topic. What does *most* of the good research say over the last ten to twenty years on topic X? Is this new study's finding in line with this larger body of knowledge? Are there other studies that support this new perspective or disagree with it? How robust are those studies? We must see how every new study compares with and contributes to what the existing reliable research says. This is precisely what we have tried to do in this book. Doing this is certainly very difficult as these are complex matters. But it's what's required to really know what the truth is.

WE MISS VITAL NUANCES

Truth is most often found in the nuances. Failing to appreciate the nuances is a very important reason why untruths get circulated so widely. I think this is often one of the biggest causes of the understanding, reception, and repeating of many such falsehoods. A statement seems solid and backed by reputable research—satisfying most good Missourians—but critical nuances are missed. As we have seen, this is very much the case in this topic. It's why the answer to "Is the church shrinking?" is both yes and no. It all depends on how and what your measuring. It is cold and uncontestable fact that churches adhering to the more liberal traditions are shrinking. People who never really had a faith to begin with but used to say they've "always attended Good Shepherd Lutheran" are more truthfully answering they are really "nothing" faith-wise. These trends are true. But it is just as true that biblical evangelical and nondenominational churches are growing quite nicely. Nuance.

So when you hear stories of the church declining, the important nuance question is "Among what churches?" Is it good news that mainline churches that are bailing on important biblical teachings are declining? Is it good news that those that are faithful to biblical teaching and practice are growing? I think it is and you likely agree. As Ed Stetzer from Wheaton College said, Christianity is not declining. It's being clarified. The sky is not falling; it's just the ground that's shifting, and in a good way, shaking out the wheat from the chaff.

Let's look at one real-life example from a few years ago of how overlooking nuance can create misunderstanding. A major initiative by good scholars at a noted evangelical seminary concluded that 40 to 50 percent of young people were leaving the church. They did indeed look at a number of sources in landing on this number and not just their own investigation, which is good. They cited a few mainstream, reliable sources and did so correctly.

- Gallup says about 40 percent of young adults who attended church when they were sixteen or seventeen years of age are no longer attending.
- LifeWay Research finds that well over 50 percent of young people who attended at least one year in a Protestant church during high school will stop attending for at least a year between the years of eighteen and twenty-two.
- The National Survey of Youth and Religion found an approximate 30 percent drop in weekly attendance by young people across multiple Protestant denominations.

Each of these stats they cited were indeed true and correct and from solid sources. But can you spot some important nuances in these statements that might challenge the "our kids are leaving the faith in droves" narrative?

Consider the Gallup and LifeWay numbers. The larger story here is the *length of time* these students attended either church or youth group. It wasn't necessarily a long time. So the conclusion should really be "Kids who don't attend church for a very long time are not likely to take that faith into adulthood." Few would find such a statement newsworthy, as its conclusion is obvious. But this is largely what these stats are saying.

The third stat is merely showing the risk across many unnamed

Protestant traditions. Were they mostly mainline churches? Mostly evangelical and nondenominational? As we learned, this is a distinction that makes all the difference.

Essentially, the conclusion from these snippets is hardly newsworthy: young people who attend various kinds of churches for short periods of time are much less likely to hang on to that faith. That is a world's difference from saying that people who grow up regularly attending a serious, Bible-based church are likely to fall away. Nuances matter.

WE STRETCH THE TRUTH

Finally, there is the simple phenomenon of holy truth-stretching. We have become much too familiar with this in the church:

"How many came to the revival last night?"

"Oh, there must have been over two hundred!" comes the reply.

And both questioner and the answerer know that's a gracious number. It's what we do, unfortunately.

We do the same with bad news as it applies to attacks and challenges to the church. "We must have gotten half a dozen negative calls about our road sign that tells people to 'get right with Jesus,'" when the actual number was precisely three and an additional caller challenged the spelling of the Savior's name. It is the rare person who doesn't feel justified in inflating numbers when it's "for the work of the kingdom." One of the executive leaders here at Focus on the Family will often ask, "Is that the actual number or the 'evange*lastic*' figure?" He's asking if we are stretching the numbers for the sake of a good ministry report.

* * *

Yes, all these details, angles, and nuances make it very confusing for all of us to discern what's true from false when all we want to do is be faithful to and active in the Lord's work. And it *is* confusing. As my research colleagues are apt to say about our work and peoples' likelihood to misinterpret the data: "These people are professionals. Don't try this at home." You do need a good bit of background knowledge and experience to pick out the meat from the bones in such research. It's why I wrote this book and why the other authors cited throughout these pages wrote up their studies as well.

The answer for this dilemma is not to become a sociologist yourself, unless you want to, but simply to find and rely on a handful of solid sources for such data. Some of the best are believers who are doing solid, academic research at secular institutions. They do exist, and their position demands they be infinitely precise in how they do their research and reach their conclusions. This has been a very reliable and fruitful approach for me in my work at Focus on the Family over the decades. Find those who regularly ask critical questions regarding these topics, those who are not quick to settle for the popular understanding of the crowd and who read widely and deeply on their topic. Follow their work and compare what you are hearing from others with what these scholars are saying.

Try this for fun. When you read about a study in the paper or on a web that seems to challenge something fundamental to your faith, look up the original study or source and read it in full. You can likely find the actual study online with little problem. You will often discover the problem or weakness between what was reported and what the source actually says rather quickly when you learn what to look for. My peers and I see it all the time in our work; we can almost always depend on it. Its been my job security for more than twenty years! Some of the discrepancies between what is reported and what the study itself actually says by any commonsense reading are astounding. Digging more deeply is something the journalist should have done, for sure. But unfortunately, few do any more, so we must.

Discernment is vital. Unfortunately, it is increasingly rare today, even in the church. It doesn't have to be this way, and it shouldn't.

CHAPTER 11

THE HOLY SPIRIT IS NOT ASLEEP AT THE WHEEL

Some good news for you about this chapter. I've saved it for last as it's the most important one in the book because its topic is more central and foundational than any other in understanding why the church is not dying and indeed, cannot die. It deals with the driving force that propels the work of the church in the world from its beginning two thousand years ago, right through today and until that glorious moment when Christ returns.

Let's begin, when we hear that the church and Christianity are taking a dramatic nosedive (if not actually dying), by asking who or what is to blame. Every failure has a cause. If your car dies on the highway, if it just stops, we know something must be wrong. Even the most mechanically ignorant person can generally deduce the general problem. It's not a flat tire. The radio hasn't gone out. It's not because the heater has stopped working. It's not because this moment is simply the end of your car's life or it just chose to stop working. We know that something has gone wrong with the engine or we've run out of gas. There has to be a cause.

Similarly, if the church has dramatically lost all power and is forced to helplessly drift over to the shoulder, we must first look at its engine, the power force that drives it forward or its fuel source, right? Asking what fuels and drives the church, how it works, and what might be wrong with it is much more important than bemoaning the loss of power. This is because the question speaks to what the fundamental nature and dynamic of the church is.

So what is the primary driver of the church in the world?

Determining where its power comes from, and understanding its nature is the most absolute evidence we need that the church universal *is not* and in fact *cannot* die or even get to the point of needing life support. Not in this age. Not ever. FULL STOP.

In fact, all the talk about a dying church is woefully ignorant of this central part of Christianity itself and it should be embarrassing to us that we tolerate it. It is why believing and repeating the Chicken Little narrative is really so troubling. Not because of what it falsely says about the current state of the church, but about what it says of the very nature of the trinitarian God of Christianity. Yes, that is a dramatic and arresting statement, I know. But let's see why it's the absolutely true.

The third person of the divine Trinity, the Holy Spirit, drives the church, directing, animating, and empowering it in every age. Embracing a Chicken Little view of the fate of the church in the world today rests on an extremely faulty theology of the Holy Spirit, what theologians call *pneumatology*. It's important we know the meaning of this term. We know *-ology* means "the study of," such as biology, zoology, and theology. But what about *pneuma*? It's a Greek word (πνεῦμα) that appears around 385 times in the New Testament; 105 times in the Gospels. Understanding the meanings of this word is essential to our investigation here.

Pneuma puts into our minds the images of spirit, wind, breath, power, and even life or life force. Essentially, to blow. A mechanic might think of a pneumatic tool, which is an extremely powerful device driven by air to move incredibly heavy objects or an impossibly tight lug nut with remarkable torque. It speaks of extraordinary power, something to be treated with great respect and care. As breath, it is remarkably animating. When we think of a person who has "gotten the Holy Spirit," we do not think of a quiet, contemplative person or someone at rest. We think of someone who is dramatically enlivened with great energy. They simply cannot be ignored, can they?

The Holy Spirit, as *pneuma*, is the most powerful life-giving agent, and He is presented to us as a divine person in Genesis 1:2 and John 3:8, for it is the *Spirit* that gives both life and new life.

In fact, the ancient Nicene Creed, that statement that helps all believers know and confess true Christian orthodoxy through the ages, tells us the Holy Spirit is "the Lord, the giver of life." Just as emergency personnel will work to blow breath into a person who is showing no signs of life, the Holy Spirit blows His breathe of life into us, as well as into His church. He gives us life, and we cannot live, grow, or act without it. And more importantly, we cannot *not* live, grow and act when it is blown upon us. To say it is effectual by its very nature is an incredible understatement.

This truth gets us to our relevant point. The Holy Spirit blows His life into His church continuously. He can't *not* do it, for it is His very essence to do so. As long as a rose is a rose, it will have a wonderful fragrance. Water will always be wet. So it is with the Holy Spirit. He doesn't give life here and there when needed and then get back to doing whatever it is He really takes divine joy in doing. This is who He is, the one who gives divine power, life, animation. I hope this truth helps you get the gist of where we are going here.

If the church is indeed dying in this age, how could its driver, the source of its life and spirit, let it do so? He cannot. And that is the point.

The Holy Spirit is *not* and *can never* be asleep at the wheel. He is relentless, and thus, so is His church, which is the Father, Son, and Holy Spirit's body in the world. That body can become ill, to be sure, and it does. *But it cannot die and it never will.* That would be absolutely contrary to the very character and nature of the Holy Spirit Himself. If we believe the church can die, and is in fact doing so, as far too many good people are claiming, we have a terrible theology of the Holy Spirit. Perhaps even a heretical one. That cannot stand.

WHO IS THE HOLY SPIRIT?

Jesus promises us in the second half of John 14 that He will ask the Father to send us another Helper. First, think about the cooperative Trinitarian dynamic at work here: God the Son will ask God the Father to send the gift of God the Holy Spirit to His church to be with us forever! Jesus promises us that the Holy Spirit will guide us into all truth, teaching us all things and reminding us what Jesus has said to us. This provision of truth is also the provision of life, for Christ came to testify to the truth and to give us life and life more abundant.

The foundational part of Christian theology is understanding the relationship between the persons of the Godhead. Was Jesus created by the Father? When did the Holy Spirit become the Holy Spirit? The early fathers of the church worked all of these important questions out with great care, and they put them into foundational creeds for the church to recite, study, and remember in order to understand and live out right Christian belief. The creed that gives us the best understanding of the nature of the Holy Spirit in relation to the Father and Son is the Nicene Creed, which came from the Council of Nicaea in AD 325. Concerning the Holy Spirit, all true Christians proclaim, hopefully weekly,

I believe in the Holy Spirit, the Lord, the giver of life,
who proceeds from the Father and the Son,
who with the Father and the Son is adored and glorified,
who has spoken through the prophets.

Consider this very essential but little understood phrase: "who proceeds from the Father and the Son." This is critical. Before anything existed, before the foundation of the world, there was a Father loving a Son and a Son loving a Father. This was and is the most powerful and consequential love between two persons that has ever existed and will ever exist. It is the most beautiful, powerful and original force in all of reality. That love, being so powerful, so substantive, and so divine, is brought forth into reality in a third divine person, the Holy Spirit. Their love is manifest in real divine life, character, and personality. The Holy proceeds from the divinized, personized love of the Father and Son, proceeding naturally and eternally from them.

As the great Saint Augustine taught us, the Trinity is a community of love, consisting of three beings, the Lover, the Loved, and Love Himself: Father, Son, and Holy Spirit. Since they have always loved one another without beginning, increase, or decline, the Holy Spirit has always proceeded from them and will continue to as long as that love between Father and Son remains. Of course, that is forever. And that love is graciously poured out upon the world.

When someone is promised a gift, as Jesus promised His followers in John 14 that they would be sent a Helper, the question he will naturally ask is, when will it be delivered? This is the next important question we must ask about the nature of the Holy Spirit and His role in the life of the church. As most of you will know, we are given the answer in Acts 2:1–4.

Early one morning, during the earliest days of the church that Jesus founded, the apostles and many with them were all together in one room. The Scriptures do not tell us what they were doing there or who exactly was there. That is not the point of the story. The point is that in the midst of this gathering of the Savior's early followers, a great sound suddenly and surprisingly came down upon them from heaven. The Scriptures say it was like a mighty and blowing *wind*, a *pneuma* if you will. It was animating, to be sure, and dramatically changed the dynamic of that room. In fact, this wind filled the entire house, we are told, and brought what appeared to be emblems of fire resting upon the heads of each one there. The text curiously calls them "tongues as of fire" in verse 3. In verse 4, the source of this wind and its accompanying fire is given: the Holy Spirit.

The coming of the Holy Spirit upon the first believers formed Christ's church. That simple sentence is extremely profound and worth reading many times. It explains one of the most important events in the life of the church, right along with the birth, death, and resurrection of Christ, for it sent the history of the world in a new direction. The Holy Spirit empowered this small ragtag group of humble and otherwise powerless individuals to do remarkable and incredibly miraculous, totally world-changing things. The Spirit gave them voice and utterance to speak boldly in foreign languages, languages none of them had any training in, which allowed them to go and speak to *all* the world what they heard from Jesus without the problem of language translation. It was the provision of the Holy Spirit that had been spoken about by the prophet Isaiah in chapter 55, verse 11:

> So shall my word be that goes out from my mouth;
>   it shall not return to me empty,
> but it shall accomplish that which I purpose,
> and shall succeed in the thing for which I sent it.

Read that verse in light of the glum news going around today on the future of the church. Look at two key phrases here: "it shall accomplish" and "shall succeed." These are absolute and confident terms. And it was God who said these two things would happen and God cannot be wrong or mistaken. In fact, it is this very truth that is all that is really needed to bust the myth that the church is dying or could ever die.

God's personified love was poured out upon humanity, and the church was started right there in that room, early one morning in Jerusalem. He promised His word will not return empty and that the Holy Spirit will accomplish and succeed at what the Father unleashed Him to do.

We read in Acts 2:6 that the sound of the wind and the voices it empowered were so powerful and inviting that it spilled out into the streets. The various voices the Holy Spirit gave to these believers were curious to all who heard them. You see, just like New York or London today, Jerusalem was a very cosmopolitan city, and people were always there from lands the world over, each speaking their own native language. The church, with the Holy Spirit working in these motley few, immediately became a polyglot movement. It began to operate in that moment in many languages. Strangers from every country were hearing these Galileans, who were known to be of limited education, speaking clearly and eloquently in these visitors' own languages.

What were they saying? The Scriptures tell us they were telling all these foreigners about "the mighty works of God."[1] So the first movement of the Holy Spirit in the church was the rousting of this small group from their secret room, out into the streets of Jerusalem, giving them voice and boldness to speak the good news of Jesus to all nations, and He has not ceased doing so even to this day.

He has not ceased doing so even to this day!

And He will continue to do so tomorrow and the day after until the Son returns.

During this event, the first sermon of the Christian church was preached. Peter, who not long before had denied Christ three times, got up and spoke boldly. He didn't do it in his own power and strength but by the power and strength of the Spirit. Peter's words were the first proclamation by the Christian church of who Christ is and what He has done for mankind. Wouldn't it have been wonderful to have been there to hear Peter on that day? The Scriptures say in Acts 2:37–39 that all who heard Peter's sermon "were cut to the heart" and asked what they should do in response to this truth. Without hesitation, Peter told them,

> Repent and be baptized every one of you in the name of Jesus Christ for the forgiveness of your sins, and you will receive the gift of the Holy Spirit. For the promise is for you and for your children and for all who are far off, everyone whom the Lord our God calls to himself.

This is the gospel of Jesus Christ, the first and most basic message of Christianity. It was initiated by the coming of the Holy Spirit, inspired by the Holy Spirit, and delivered by the Holy Spirit through Peter's lungs and voice. And it became effectual in the hearts of every listener through the Holy Spirit. The Spirit is the means by which the world did, has, and will continue to receive the life-giving words of the gospel that we are told *cannot* fail in their mission. He is truly the main player on the stage that is the work and vitality of the church throughout history. And the very last verse of Acts chapter 2 is what this book you are reading is all about:

And the Lord added to their number day by day those who were being saved.

"Added to their number day by day."

If we understand anything about the church, it must be this: It was initiated by God the Father, who sent the Son. It was founded by the Son, who gave His life as a ransom for all, which is the good news. It is the Holy Spirit, promised by the Son, sent by the Father, who dispersed, empowered, equipped, emboldened, and animated the church. He breathed life into it, giving it the power, direction, and comfort of His Spirit. And it didn't just happen at Pentecost and stop there, as if God gave it a good kickstart and let it go under its own power. Just as breath must constantly be drawn into our lungs—moment by moment, without interruption—the Holy Spirit literally, actually, pumps life and life-giving power into the lungs of the church. The church then exhales that life-giving breath out into the world.

The Holy Spirit does so without ceasing and has since that morning on Pentecost, at every place the church has ever gone, in every age. He did so last week and yesterday, and He will continue to do so today, tomorrow, next month, and until the culmination of time. This fact describes the very nature of what the church *is* today.

Given this, we must recall what Jesus said regarding the foundation of His church. This involved Peter here as well, and Jesus's words are given to us in Matthew 16:15–18.

Jesus asked His disciples who they believed He was. Peter famously spoke up and proclaimed so beautifully and accurately, "You are the Christ, the Son of the living God." Jesus responded strongly to Peter's confession: "Blessed are you, Simon Bar-Jonah! For flesh and blood has not revealed this to you, but my Father who is in heaven." He then explained that it would be upon this rock-solid proclamation of Peter's that He would establish His church, "and the gates of hell shall not prevail against it." *The gates of hell shall not prevail against it.* What does this mean exactly?

It is a curious statement, and theologians have offered a few different explanations, which we will not get into here. But most agree that the "hell" spoken of in this verse is the place of death. Thus death, which is Satan's domain, will not prevail against His church.

Death will not prevail upon Jesus, which He speaks of right after He makes this statement. He says He will die and rise again from the grave, the ultimate victory over death and hell. But this verse also speaks of the church, which will never suffer the effects of death. It will not and never be overcome, thwarted, slowed down, or weakened. It will never be prevailed against. If the church were indeed dying today, that would mean it was being prevailed against, thwarted, and weakened. Jesus not only promises this will never happen, but He says that it can't. The death of the church would either render our Lord a liar or terribly confused. It should have long been clear to us what those spreading the Chicken Little news have unwittingly been saying about Jesus's character and the Holy Spirit's agency.

Christ's bride cannot *not* grow. Its Author is life. Its Savior is life, and its Life-giver is life. Divine life moves only in one direction. Toward more, abundant life. Death and decline are its exact opposite. Thus, the church cannot be thwarted. Yes, local manifestations of it can grow complacent and get off track. Local churches can grow lax, like the church at Laodicea mentioned in Revelation, or even lifeless, like the church of Sardis. They can be waylaid by false teachers, like the church of Pergamum. They can get seduced into sexual immorality, like the churches at Corinth and Thyatira.[2] They can become dominated by squabbling and pettiness. But the church itself cannot be hindered.

Let me leave you with two verses to consider and reflect upon as we close this book. They are historical statements marking two different times and realities for the church, one being uttered by God at the very birth of the church and one that will be uttered at her culmination. The first are the last words of Jesus recorded in the Gospels:

All authority in heaven and on earth has been given to me. Go therefore and make disciples of all nations, baptizing them in the name of the Father and of the Son and of the Holy Spirit, teaching them to observe all that I have commanded you. And behold, I am with you always, to the end of the age. (Matthew 28:18–20)

God will not and cannot walk away from the spreading of His good news, of the baptizing of new believers, of making them into new disciples. He cannot walk away from the continued growth and spread of His beloved bride, the church. It is His desire and purpose to use us and every local church to fulfill His mission. To believe it is failing today is not only *not* supported in the sociological and historical evidence, but it is terrible, if not heretical, theology. Doing so misunderstands the most intimate nature of God Himself. Thus, we need to stop saying it and correct those who do.

We know where the church is going and where it will end up. It is told to us in dramatic fashion in the last pages of Scripture.

I looked, and behold, a great multitude that no one could number, from every nation, from all tribes and peoples and languages, standing before the throne and before the Lamb, clothed in white robes, with palm branches in their hands, and crying out with a loud voice, "Salvation belongs to our God who sits on the throne, and to the Lamb!" (Revelation 7:9–10)

A great multitude that no one could number. As the cells of the body of every living person multiply every minute of every day, so do the cells that make up the body of Christ. It can't be otherwise. Should we repent for believing otherwise?

Amen and amen.

CONCLUSION
WHAT THE FUTURE REQUIRES

So . . . We've learned a bunch of important and surprising truths through these pages. Let's summarize the ten most fundamental facts we should remember.

1. Christianity is shrinking in the mainline churches. They are tanking as if they have a millstone around their necks. And perhaps they do. It's because they left biblical Christianity decades ago and continue to with great passion. ·

2. Christianity is growing nicely in the evangelical, non-denominational, and more conservative mainline churches.

3. Christianity and Christian ministries are absolutely *exploding* around the world, particularly in China and Asia, Africa, Latin America, and Oceania. Christianity is on track to continue to grow through every decade of the twenty-first century.

4. The nones are not a new or growing group of nonbelievers. They do not signify a shift in belief but in categorization.

This group is merely admitting they never really had any faith to begin with.

5. Teens and young adults are *not* leaving the church in droves. They've left the mainline churches, as others are doing. But they are hanging strong, and indeed growing significantly in biblically faithful, vibrant churches that are calling them to real discipleship.

6. Young people raised with a living, real faith in their teen years are almost guaranteed to successfully carry that faith into adulthood. Parents are the primary influence here.

7. Ministries that work with teens and college students are seeing unprecedented growth today and have over the last few decades, growing larger than they ever have. And this at the very time buses of young people were supposed to have been leaving hourly for the land of unbelief.

8. Those churches that are changing their beliefs "to get with the times" by liberalizing their sexual mores, tossing things like the reality of sin, miracles, and the divinity of Christ overboard, are certainly not attracting new believers. Especially the young. The irony of the so-called "welcoming and affirming" churches regarding homosexuality is that people are leaving them, including those who identify as same-sex attracted.

9. Christian parents who want to build a lifelong faith in their children need to do only a few important things. Doing so is not rocket science or a secret formula that must be applied *just* right. Your chances of success are remarkably high.

10. Finally, it's the Holy Spirit who runs and drives Christ's church across time and throughout the nations. He is unstoppable, unquenchable, and inherently life-giving. He is not nodding off, sickly, or on vacation. The work of His heart and very character will not be thwarted. He is God. To believe the church is dying is to deny these truths and judge God either confused or a liar.

This is the state of the church today in the United States and in much of the world. The places where it is not growing are relatively rare and small. To be sure, not everything with the church is all positive. It has its problems because it consists of people like me who have their problems. But as we pointed out, this has always been the nature of the church. Perhaps the only golden age of the church was that day of Pentecost. After that, one only needs to read the letters of Paul and the first few chapters of Revelation to see it was not all super-duper.

But this much is true about the church today and in every age. If you take just one thing away from this book, it should be this:

Jesus's church has and will continue to move through history and humanity like a freight train because it is empowered by the infinite drive of the Holy Spirit to radically save and redeem lives and transform communities, even nations. The Holy Spirit is the most powerful force in the universe. Thus, so is the church that He empowers.

If we consult Scripture about what we must do as individual Christians and leaders in the church today, we find that what we learn there is backed up in the research from current sociology of religion and impressively so. We must:

- Submit ourselves in obedience to the loving guidance and power of the Holy Spirit and the salvific work of Christ and His lordship.
- Commit ourselves to living out the new life that God gives us in the community where we live in both practical and supernatural ways.
- Preach, teach, and live out the truth and beauty of Scripture in obedient and faithful ways.
- Apply God's Word in new ways to the people in our age, but never rewrite its truths to accommodate the spirit of the age. The last liberalizing century of church history shows us that doing so returns utterly void.
- Make vibrant, alive worship a regular part of our church life. Conduct it as if we *really* believe God is present and doing great things among us.
- Welcome *all* and everyone to our churches with absolute grace and eagerness, especially when they actually take the trouble to walk through our doors.
- Provide resources and groups that meet the felt needs present in our communities, things like food and clothes closets; divorce and substance-abuse recovery groups;

premarital and marriage education programs; single-parent helps; and other such things.

- Reach out to, encourage, and even call out for correction those who are presenting a rewritten gospel that denies fundamental things the church has taught biblically and faithfully throughout history. (If you don't believe such a thing has a place in the church, read the Gospels and New Testament letters again.)

- Continue to faithfully and lovingly take God's life-giving gospel to all peoples wherever they might be found in this beautiful world.

People will be drawn to these things because a church that does them is being obedient to who God *is* and what He *has been* doing from day one. Their deepest and most personal human needs will be met: for life, for truth, for love, for redemption. These things have been and will continue to be irresistible. How can they not? God's Word will not return void. What the Bible says of the church on its first day will also be true of these churches today:

And the Lord added to their number day by day those who were being saved. (Acts 2:47)

Church, be of good cheer. God is true. Aslan is on the move. Chicken Little is mistaken. God's future is bright. It cannot be otherwise.

ENDNOTES

Chapter 1: Is Chicken Little Right?

1   Is Chicken Little a boy or a girl? Two tellings of the story by Disney, one in 1943 and the second in 2005, have him as a boy. But the classic stories dating back to the early 1800s have her as a girl. I've chosen her as a girl. You can pick the gender you wish, which seems to be all the rage today.

2   In references like these, I chose not to mention the names of the Christian leaders making such statements for obvious reasons: It is bad manners to point out the mistakes of others by name. Do to others as you would want done to yourself. But they are real statements made by real people and organizations.

3   Brent Staples, "If You're Devout, Get Out!," *New York Times Review of Books*, November 26, 2000.

4   Christian Smith, "Evangelicals Behaving Badly with Statistics," *Books & Culture*, January/February 2007.

Chapter 2: The Truth Is Much More Hopeful Than You Think

1   Ed Stetzer, "Religion in America: An Interview with Greg Smith of the Pew Research Center (Part 2)," Christianitytoday.com, January 29, 2016.

2   Ed Stetzer, "The Present and Future of Evangelicalism: An Interview with Dr. Rodney Stark," Christiantytoday.com, June 9, 2015.

3   Landon Schnabel and Sean Bock, "The Persistent and Exceptional Intensity of American Religion: A Response to Recent Research," *Sociological Science* (4) 2017: 686–700, emphasis added.

4   Ibid., emphasis added.

5   Mainline churches are those of the older denominations like Episcopal, certain kinds of Presbyterian, Lutheran, Methodist, and others. The denominations themselves are not doing well in terms of attendance, but there are certain branches of them that are doing quite well. These are typically, to a congregation, the more traditional and conservative ones.

6   https://www.youtube.com/watch?v=XcViApak4Zg, accessed February 13, 2019.

7   Landon Schnabel and Sean Bock, "The Persistent and Exceptional Intensity of American Religion."

8   Ibid. Although they use the general term *religion*, they mean Christianity, as one's view of the Bible is one of their three measures of religious vitality.

9   It can be found at https://gssdataexplorer.norc.org/trends.

10 Each of the measures and categories presented here from the GSS saw movements both up and down over the decades, but they each showed overall stability or a slight increase from 1970 to today.

11 *America's Changing Religious Landscape*, Pew Research Center, May 12, 2015.

12 Ibid., 9.

13 Ibid., 14. It went from 26.3 percent of the US population down to 25.4 percent.

14 Ibid., 21.

15 Personal communication between myself and Professor Kosmin, August 14, 2018.

16 *America's Changing Religious Landscape*, 26.

Chapter 3: The Explosive Growth of "the Nons"
1   *America's Changing Religious Landscape*, Pew Research Center, May 12, 2015, 32.
2   James 2:17
3   *U.S. Public Becoming Less Religious: Modest Drop in Overall Rates of Belief and Practice, but Religiously Affiliated Americans Are as Observant as Before*, Pew Research Center, November 2015, 6.
4   *Status of Global Christianity, 2017, in the Context of 1900–2050*, Center for the Study of Global Christianity at Gordon-Conwell Theological Seminary (2018).
5   John 14:6
6   Mark 9:31

Chapter 4: The Nones Are Not New
1   Ed Stetzer, "Survey Fail—Christianity Isn't Dying," *USA Today*, May 3, 2015.
2   *America's Changing Religious Landscape*, Pew Research Center, May 12, 2015, 116.
3   Rodney Stark, *The Triumph of Faith: Why the World Is More Religious Than Ever* (ISI Books, 2015), 190, emphasis in original.
4   Landon Schnabel and Sean Bock, "The Persistent and Exceptional Intensity of American Religion: A Response to Recent Research," *Sociological Science* (4) 2017, 690.
5   *Faith in Flux: Changes in Religious Affiliation in the U.S.*, the Pew Forum on Religion & Public Life, April 2009, 4.
6   Personal communication between Professor Kosmin and myself, August 14, 2018.

Chapter 5: Stick a Fork in It: The Major Fail of Liberal Christianity
1   David M. Barnes and Ilan H. Meyer, "Religious Affiliation, Internalized Homophobia, and Mental Health in Lesbians, Gay Men and Bisexuals," *American Journal of Orthopsychiatry* 82 (2012): 505–515.
2   *America's Changing Religious Landscape*, Pew Research Center, May 12, 2015, 87.
3   Roger Finke and Rodney Stark, *The Churching of America, 1776–2005: Winners and Losers in Our Religious Economy* (Rutgers University Press, 2005).
4   David Millard Haskell, et al., "Theology Matters: Comparing the Traits of Growing and Declining Mainline Protestant Church Attendees and Clergy," *Review of Religious Research* (58) 2016: 515–541.
5   Ecclesiastes 1:9
6   David M. Kelley, *Why Conservative Churches Are Growing: A Study in Sociology of Religion* (Mercer University Press, 1972), 1, 25–26.

Chapter 6: How Is Christianity Doing Globally?
1   Philip Jenkins, "Christianity's New Center," *The Atlantic*, September 2002.
2   Alvin Schmidt, *How Christianity Changed the World* (Zondervan, 2004); Rodney Stark, *The Victory of Reason: How Christianity Led to Freedom, Capitalism, and Western Success* (Random House, 2006).
3   Philip Jenkins, *The New Faces of Christianity, Believing the Bible in the Global South* (Oxford University Press, 2006), 5.
4   Philip Jenkins, *The Next Christendom: The Coming of Global Christianity* (Oxford University Press, 2002), 9.
5   John Shelby Spong, *Why Christianity Must Change or Die* (HarperCollins, 1999).
6   Philip Jenkins, "Christianity's New Center."
7   Philip Jenkins, *The Next Christendom*, 2; Philip Jenkins, *The New Faces of Christianity*, 99.
8   Philip Jenkins, "The Next Christianity," *The Atlantic*, October 2002.
9   Philip Jenkins, *The Next Christendom*, 2.

10 According to the Center for the Study of Global Christianity, Gordon-Conwell Theological Seminary, the global number of Catholics in the world is 120 percent greater today than the total number of all Protestants. It is expected to be 111 percent greater by 2025.

11 Philip Jenkins, *The Next Christendom*, 7.

12 *Status of Global Christianity, 2017, in the Context of 1900–2050*, Center for the Study of Global Christianity at Gordon-Conwell Theological Seminary (2018).

13 Philip Jenkins, *The Next Christendom*, 9.

14 Ibid., 8.

15 Andrew Brown, "The Anglican Schism Over Sexuality Marks the End of a Global Church," *Guardian*, January 8, 2016.

16 Personal interview with John Stonestreet, September 13, 2018.

17 Quoted in Philip Jenkins, *The New Faces of Christianity*, 1.

18 Philip Jenkins, *The New Faces of Christianity*, 15.

19 Quoted in Ethan Vesely-Flad, "For the Soul of the Church," *ColorLines*, March 21, 2005.

20 Philip Jenkins, *The Next Christendom*, 8.

21 Ibid., 13.

22 Rodney Stark, *The Triumph of Faith: Why the World Is More Religious Than Ever* (ISI Books, 2015), 126.

23 "Obituary: God," *Economist*, December 23, 1999.

24 John Micklethwait and Adrian Wooldridge, *God Is Back: How the Global Revival of Faith is Changing the World* (Penguin Press, 2009), 6.

25 Eleanor Albert, "Christianity in China," Backgrounder by the Council on Foreign Relations, last update March 9, 2018.

26 Zhang Boli, presentation at conference, "Christianity in China: A Force for Change?," the Brookings Institution, Washington, DC, June 3, 2014.

27 Ibid.

28 John Micklethwait and Adrian Wooldridge, *God Is Back*, 12.

29 Ibid.

30 Ibid., 25.

31 *The Changing Global Religious Landscape*, Pew Research Center, April 5, 2017, 4–8.

32 Eric Kaufmann, *Shall the Religious Inherit the Earth?: Demography and Politics in the Twenty-First Century* (Profile Books, 2010), xv.

33 David Bentley Hart, "Freedom and Decency," *First Things*, June 2004.

Chapter 7: Are Young People Really Leaving the Church?

1 Ed Stetzer, "The Present and Future of Evangelicalism: An Interview with Dr. Rodney Stark," Christianitytoday.com, June 9, 2015.

2 Rodney Stark, *What Americans Really Believe: New Findings from the Baylor Surveys of Religion* (Baylor University Press, 2008), 11.

3 Bradley R. E. Wright, *Christians Are Hate-Filled Hypocrites . . . and Other Lies You've Been Told* (Bethany House, 2010), 65.

4 Byron Johnson, "The Good News About Evangelicalism," *First Things*, February 2011, 14.

5 Christian Smith, *Souls in Transition: The Religious and Spiritual Lives of Emerging Adults* (Oxford University Press, 2009), 95, 99.

6 Ibid., 141, emphasis added.

7 Lisa D. Pearce and Melinda Lundquist Denton, *A Faith of Their Own: Stability and Change in the Religiosity of America's Adolescents* (Oxford University Press, 2011), 116, 163, 167.

8   *Millennials: A Portrait of Generation Next*, Pew Research Center, February 2010, 85.

9   *Millennials: A Portrait of Generation Next*, 88–91.

10 *Faith in Flux: Changes in Religious Affiliation in the U.S.*, the Pew Forum on Religion & Public Life, April 2009, 4.

11 Christian Smith, *Souls in Transition*, 223.

Chapter 8: Passing Faith to Our Kids Is Neither a Crapshoot nor Rocket Science

1   Vern Bengtson, *Families and Faith: How Religion Is Passed Down Across Generations* (Oxford University Press, 2013), 184.

2   Ibid., 185 (emphasis added).

3   Quoted in David Briggs, "Parents No. 1 Influence Helping Teens Remain Religiously Active as Young Adults," *Association of Religious Data Archives*, October 29, 2014.

4   Christian Smith, *Souls in Transition: The Religious and Spiritual Lives of Emerging Adults* (Oxford University Press, 2009), 223.

5   Scott M. Myers, "An Interactive Model of Religiosity Inheritance: The Importance of Family Context," *American Sociological Review* (61) 1996: 858–866, emphasis in original.

6   Norella M. Putney, "The Transmission of Religion Across Generations: How Ethnicity Matters," chapter 10 in Merrill Silverstein and Roseann Giarrusso, eds., *Kinship and Cohort in an Aging Society: From Generation to Generation* (Johns Hopkins University Press, 2013), 212.

7   Christopher D. Bader and Scott A. Desmond, "Do as I Say and as I Do: The Effects of Consistent Parental Beliefs and Behaviors upon Religious Transmission," *Sociology of Religion* (67) 2006: 313–329.

8   The information presented here on the most important and consequential things successful parents do comes from both Bengtson's and Smith's works. The primary source, though, is Smith's *Souls in Transition*, particularly pages 217–228.

9   Mark D. Regnerus and Jeremy E. Uecker, "Finding Faith, Losing Faith: The Prevalence and Context of Religious Transformations During Adolescence," *Review of Religious Research*, 2006, volume 47(3), 217–37.

Chapter 9: "Is My Church Shrinking?" and Other Questions to Consider

1   Shawna L. Anderson et al., "Dearly Departed: How Often Do Congregations Close?," *Journal for the Scientific Study of Religion* (47) 2008: 321–328.

2   *Young Life Annual Reports*, 2014 and 2017.

3   *360° InterVarsity Annual Report*, 2016–2017.

4   Richard J. Murnane and Sean F. Reardon, "Long-Term Trends in Private School Enrollment by Family Income," *AERA Open* (4) 2018: 1–24.

5   Farran Powell and Briana Boyington, "Why Enrollment Is Rising at Large Christian Colleges," *U.S. News & World Report*, December 6, 2017.

6   *Current Term Enrollment Estimates: Spring 2017*, National Student Clearinghouse Research Center, May 23, 2017, Table 1.

7   George Marsden, "A Renaissance of Christian Higher Education in the United States," in Joel Carpenter et al., eds., *Christian Higher Education: A Global Reconnaissance* (Eerdmans Publishing Co. 2014), 257.

8   Joel Carpenter et al., eds., *Christian Higher Education: A Global Reconnaissance*, 16.

9   *Status of Global Christianity, 2017, in the Context of 1900–2050*, Center for the Study of Global Christianity at Gordon-Conwell Theological Seminary (2018).

10 "Book Publishing Annual StatShot Survey Reveals Religious Crossover and Inspirational Books Supported Trade Book Growth in 2016," press release from the Association of American Publishers, August 1, 2017.

11 Jim Milliot, "Trade Sales Were a Bright Spot in a Dark Year for Sales: Industry Sales Fell 5.1% in 2016 from 2015," *Publishers Weekly*, August 4, 2017.

12 Jim Milliot, "For Publishers, 2018 Is Off to a Decent Start," *Publishers Weekly*, May 18, 2018.

13 *Status of Global Christianity, 2017, in the Context of 1900–2050*.

14 Ibid.

15 Simon G. Brauer, "How Many Congregations Are There? Updating a Survey-Based Estimate," *Journal for the Scientific Study of Religion* (56) 2017: 438–448.

16 Scott Thumma and Warren Bird, "Recent Shifts in America's Largest Protestant Churches: Megachurch 2015 Report," *Leadership Network & Hartford Institute*, 2015, 9–10.

Chapter 11: The Holy Spirit Is Not Asleep at the Wheel

1 Acts 2:11

2 These, save for Corinth, are the churches mentioned in chapters 2 and 3 of Revelation.

ABOUT THE AUTHOR

GLENN T. STANTON is the director of Global Family Formation Studies at Focus on the Family, where he has worked since 1993. In this capacity he does extensive sociological, anthropological, and theological research on the family as an essential societal institution. He debates and lectures extensively on the issues of gender, sexuality, marriage, and parenting at universities and churches around the world.

Stanton is the author of eight books on the issues of marriage, gender, and the family. His latest are *Loving My LGBT Neighbor: Being Friends in Grace and Truth* and *The Ring Makes All the Difference: The Hidden Consequences of Cohabitation and the Strong Benefits of Marriage.* He is a regular columnist for various blogs and a senior contributor to the *Federalist.* He served the George W. Bush administration for many years as a consultant on increasing fatherhood involvement in the Head Start program.

He is also the cowriter of *Irreplaceable*, a film seen in theatres nationwide, and the coauthor and creator of *The Family Project*, a twelve-session small group DVD curriculum produced by Focus on the Family. Stanton earned bachelor's degrees in philosophy, communication arts, and religion, and a master's degree in philosophy, history, and religion from the University of West Florida.

He enjoys reading, mountain biking (a bit too fast), hiking the trails of Colorado, and fly-fishing its rivers; and he still skateboards the ramps and pools at his local skatepark, yet less radically than in years past.

glenntstanton.com

31901064802988